ROAR SOFTLY
and Carry a Great Lipstick

D0048393

ROAR SOFTLY
and Carry a Great Lipstick

---

28 Women Writers on
Life, Sex, and Survival

Edited by Autumn Stephens

Inner Ocean Publishing, Inc.
Maui, Hawai'i • San Francisco, California

Inner Ocean Publishing, Inc.
P.O. Box 1239
Makawao, Maui, HI 96768-1239
www.innerocean.com

Printed on recycled paper.

Cover design: sparklecreative
Book design: Madonna Gauding

Lyrics from "Be Like a Bird" by Arthur Frackenpohl
Copyright © Neil A. Kjos Music Company
Reprinted with permission 2004

PUBLISHER CATALOGING-IN-PUBLICATION DATA

Roar softly and carry a great lipstick : 28 women writers on life, sex, and survival / edited by Autumn Stephens. —Makawao, HI : Inner Ocean, 2004.
    p. ; cm.
    ISBN: 1-930722-38-9 (pbk.)
    1. Women—Anecdotes. 2. Women—Identity. 3. Women—
    Psychology. 4. Self-esteem in women. 5. Sex role—Anecdotes.
    6. Feminism—Anecdotes. I. Stephens, Autumn, 1956- II. Title.

HQ1206 .R63 2004
305.4--dc22   0411

Distributed by Publishers Group West

For information on promotions, bulk purchases, premiums, or educational use, please contact Special Markets: 866.731.2216 or sales@innerocean.com.

I am my own heroine.

—Marie Bashkirtseff

Contents

Introduction

There are many survival stories about men. Man vs. whale. Man. vs. bull. Man vs. every law of nature you have ever heard of— piloting a ship into an ice-bound sea, for example, or buck-jumping a motorcycle across the Snake River Canyon, or scaling Mount Everest in a storm. Those stories are interesting, to be sure, the stuff of block-busters, and freshman literature classes, and this morning's newspaper headlines. But *Roar Softly and Carry a Great Lipstick* (the title riffs, of course, on Theodore Roosevelt's macho motto: "Walk softly and carry a big stick") is about a different kind of story. *Roar Softly* is a book about what—and how—*women* survive.

On these pages, twenty-eight contemporary writers—not merely professionally accomplished, but courageous and clear-sighted wit-nesses to their own lives—recount their *mano a mano* tussles with trouble. Bodies that betrayed them. Obsessions that plagued them. Loved ones who left them. Good fortune that eluded them. Self-revealing but not self-pitying, these are candid, firsthand accounts of facing down the aggravations—as slight as yet another magazine fea-ture on toning fleshy thighs, as shattering as a mother's death—that unsettle women, or unnerve us, or drive us stark raving mad. These are stories about strength of character, and clarity of mind, and the emo-tional alchemy through which we transform the dross of despair into something golden and good. And not a whale—or for that matter, an airborne motorcycle—in the bunch.

In compiling this anthology, I wanted to provide a forum for women to speak the truth, raw or unflattering as it might be, about issues that irked them, conflicts that consumed them. And I wanted readers, by association, to intuit that their own struggles were neither *sui generis* nor too shameful to divulge. But what, exactly, *was* that hypothetical "truth"? So that my preconceived notions would not unduly influence the writers whom I invited to contribute, I provided only a wisp of guidance—simply the instruction to write about overcoming "a typical life challenge for an American woman today."

One by one, over the course of several months, the essays washed up in my e-mail inbox, their tenor ranging from deliciously, edgily humorous to hell-and-back harrowing. Some were wonderfully spare and elegant; others meatier, more robust. Still others were like wine spritzers—witty, bubbling with vital frisson. Each was important and true in its own way. Each was like a message in a bottle: *Hello, anyone there? Listen! What a story I have to tell!* Trying to hold them all in my consciousness at once, hefting them in my mind, I was awed by their collective weight. The almost tangible power of so many tales of trouble confronted and transcended, obstacles overcome or ingeniously reframed. No woman was an island. Together, we were an archipelago; together, we were a goddamn continent.

Surviving anorexia. Shrugging off the ravages of middle age. Coping with physical disability. Toughing out postpartum depression. Transcending fear of authority. Rejecting motherhood. Resisting marriage. Mourning a loved one. Ruing missed opportunities. Fighting infertility. Embracing lesbianism. Fleeing an abusive spouse. Clinging tightly to cherished friends. Buying a house on a womanly, writerly salary. And, oh yes, desperately seeking sex—at twenty, or forty, or fifty. Sobering topics, most of these. But, of course, no story—no story of interest, anyway—is entirely synonymous with its topic. *Moby Dick* is not, after all, *really* about man vs. whale, any more than an essay about self-starvation is really about woman vs. bathroom scale. Like the humble pantry staples that a chef transforms into a masterful meal, the ordinary ordeals that underlay the *Roar Softly* essays were merely the prosaic ingredients of bigger, richer, more piquant dramas.

Dramas from which we could, if we paid proper attention, learn not only about women, but about ourselves, and about the different paths that we all—male and female alike—might choose as we make our way through the world.

"Sentences that begin with 'all women' are never, never true," wrote Margaret Culkin Banning (who solved *her* most pressing problem—how to single-handedly support her children—by power-writing forty books). And, indeed, just as no one issue was common to all contributors, so there was no universal solution. But as I studied these essays more closely, an interesting pattern began to emerge. With few exceptions, the strategies that women employed to resolve their difficulties had this in common: they were every bit as sex-specific as the difficulties themselves. More indirect than confrontational. More circuitous than head-on. More unifying than divisive. And, sometimes, more metaphorical than concrete. Perhaps—to pursue the Teddy Roosevelt metaphor—wielding that big stick, cowing others (or themselves) into submission, didn't feel comfortable to these essayists. Perhaps it wasn't an effective technique for them. Or perhaps women just don't tend to think in "man vs. whale" terms. In any event, I found the problem-solving strategies that the writers *did* employ so intriguing that I organized the book into sections to reflect them: Connection, Attitude Adjustment, Mind Over Matter, Problem? What Problem?, and Perseverance. This was, admittedly, a rather straightforward, "big stick" approach: in true nonlinear fashion, many essayists did not limit themselves to one technique alone. In such cases, I simply placed the piece where it seemed to fit best.

"Connection" reflects the sensibility of the numerous essayists who described turning to others in times of trouble. As a widely publicized study by psychologists at the University of California, Los Angeles recently proposed, women aren't, like men, biologically predisposed to the "flight-or-fight" response when danger threatens. Instead, our ass-saving behavior tends toward the "tend-and-befriend" model: hunker down, nurture the hell out of the young'uns (maybe they'll survive if you don't), and form protective affiliations with others. Of course, "danger," twenty-first-century style, is more apt to appear in the guise of a life-disrupting event than that of a saber-toothed tiger. Her mother's death from breast cancer, for example, prompted essayist Elizabeth Fishel to forge tighter bonds with the women in a writing group she facilitated. Not only did focusing her attention outward help Fishel climb out of depression, as she notes in "Writing for the Cure," but it also led to the entire group self-publishing a book that became a local best-seller. Taking the concept of "befriending" to a new, philanthropic level, the multiple coauthors then donated the proceeds to breast cancer research. While other writers, like Fishel, connected through structured situations such as psychotherapy and support groups, still others found solace and strength in friendship. And one essayist, Cynthia Heimel, even formed a health-restoring alliance with her dog.

Not, of course, that human behavior parts like the waters of the Continental Divide: guys (stoic, silent, primed for flight) on one side, gals (yakking and hugging) on the other. Consider, for example, Jane DeLynn's humorous, painfully honest "(Learning How to) Get Laid" and Marcelle Karp's raunchy yet amusing "Adventures in Cyber Snatching," both on the subject of pursuing casual sexual prey. Does casual sex count as connective behavior or as disconnective? Does the motive matter, or whether the pursuer is male or female? The answers to such questions, as these two intriguing explorations of nontraditional sexual roles suggest, are more ambiguous than you might think.

"Attitude Adjustment" features the work of writers who relied primarily on mental manipulations, not Rolodexes, to work through their woes. For some, simply reframing a problem cast it in a softer light. Others performed more dazzling feats of imagination. In her quirky, bittersweet "My Buddies the Oysters," Ms. Gonick describes a seemingly untenable existence: brain tumor treatments wreak havoc with her body, while post-9/11 anxiety plagues her mind. Powerless to reverse her physical deterioration, much less the course of history, Gonick ingeniously opts to alter her mental landscape. As they say, it's a woman's prerogative to change her mind. But changing one's mind in this sense is also, of course, a woman's coping mechanism. Traditionally limited to a narrow range of behavioral roles, we have soared in our imaginations—the housewife daydreaming over her laundry no less than the poet or the artist. As the perennial popularity of romance novels (or, for that matter, control-top pantyhose) suggests, fantasy still packs a powerful escapist punch.

So, apparently, do narcotics: Cheryl Strayed's "Heroin/e" is one of the most stunning, chilling pieces you will ever read about grief, and how desperately we human beings try to avoid pain. But for a quick, hangover-free upper, it's hard to beat humor—not only an instant attitude adjuster but, as noted linguist Deborah Tannen posits, a time-honored technique that women use to connect with others. You can think about that until the cows (or bulls) come home. Or you can just read Mary Roach's wry "The Marvels of Middle Age" and feel a little friendlier toward your own sagging flesh and liver spots.

In "Mind Over Matter," you'll find the work of essayists who took a spiritual approach to problem solving. It's no secret, of course, that women have customarily been the most ardent devotees of religious ritual, nor that their devotion has not, from a feminist perspective, been an altogether unmixed blessing. Looking forward to "pie in the sky" is all well and good, but what about a woman's lot in *this* life, what about "bread on the table"? Perhaps it's a reflection of our more skeptical times (skeptical of patriarchy, if not of religion) that only writer Anne Lamott emphasizes religious faith as a source of strength—and, in fact, you'll find Lamott's memorable, moving "Thirst," which also credits her recovery from alcoholism to interpersonal connections, in the first section of this book.

For other *Roar Softly* contributors, however, a distinctly free-form brand of spirituality prevailed. In her uplifting "Walking the Labyrinth with Mother," Peggy Hong describes the death-positive attitude of her Korean ancestors and the beautiful ritual she created to commemorate the anniversary of her mother's death. In "Train Sounds," Ariel Gore moves heaven and earth to buy the house that she believes will settle her restless soul. And in "Heroes of the House," Louise Rafkin transforms her potentially tedious day job as a cleaning woman into an ongoing spiritual exercise, one that entails a conscious connection with her clients (shades of "tend-and-befriend") even when they're not physically on the scene. "Sometimes I want my presence in a house to have an effect beyond that of a well-mopped floor," she writes.

Redefining problems as non-problems was the clever coping strategy of that feisty crew of contributors featured in "Problem? What Problem?" Susan B. Anthony would have been proud. For these essayists, defiant behavior that challenges the status quo is a badge of pride, not a source of shame—it is tradition, not the transgressor, that is flawed. Joyce Thompson, for example, in her terse, powerfully understated "The Flight," refuses to stand by her abusive man, while in "Just Say I Do," the fact that she has never married suggests to author Merrill Markoe only that she is discerning, not deranged. In "Naked Pictures," Sefi Atta so resents the insinuation that her young daughter's nude drawings are sinful that she overcomes her lifelong fear of authority to confront the narrow-minded principal of the girl's school. And in "Smells Like Perfume Inserts," the defiantly unglamorous Ayun Halliday takes on women's fashion magazines and reverses the charges, so to speak. "Here's one way of looking at it," Halliday writes. "Anyone who dreads bathing-suit season hasn't spent time under a burkah. If some editorially brain-dead piece of shiny can make me feel bad about my aging skin, I must not be facing chemotherapy! Comparatively speaking, I don't have a care in the world—in which case, *those fucking magazines* can be my big problem."

But sometimes there isn't an easy, or even a not-so-easy, way out. Sometimes—as many a mother-to-be has suddenly realized at the first wrenching labor pain—there is simply *no* way out. That doesn't mean, however, that the story has come to an end. "When you get to the end of your rope, tie a knot and hang on," Eleanor Roosevelt (a woman schooled in both giving birth and hanging tough) once wrote, and that is more or less what the writers in the book's final section, "Perseverance," did.

As a survival strategy, perseverance is as dull as the camouflaging coloration of a female bird. It is not, in general, the direction in which the male's action-oriented, must-dive-bomb-nest-invader-now *modus operandi* tends. But when the predator is as vast and amorphous as fate itself, whom do you dive-bomb? In what direction do you brandish that metaphorical big stick? Attempting to resolve this very problem while in a funk, Ernest Hemingway fixed things up by shooting himself in the head. By contrast, plodding old perseverance seems positively inspired. At least there's a *chance* of a happy ending.

Thus, Judith Newman doggedly pursued the goal of giving birth for years; in her essay "Baby Baby Baby Please," she leaves half a page completely blank to demonstrate the void in which she once lived. Thus, Anneli Rufus, author of the poetic, almost hallucinatory "Border Patrol," suffered a decade's worth of anorexia before finally, ambivalently beginning to eat again; even so, she writes, she lives in constant vigilance against relapse. And thus, the best-selling Haitian-born author Edwidge Danticat endured a tragic separation, through all but the earliest years of childhood, from her beloved mother. Here, in her yearning, lyrical "Legends: The Daughter," an essay-letter-poem addressed directly to her mother, Danticat retells the story of her life during those long and difficult years. "I am, as you like to say, 'trying to make art out of everything,'" she writes. "But you must know by now that this is how I have survived, that this is how I still survive."

In this, Danticat is not alone. In this, the artful rendering of hard truths, pain-to-pearls wizardry, not one of the writers whose survival stories you are about to read is alone.

Autumn Stephens

1.

Connection

The person who tries to live alone will not succeed as a human being. His heart withers if it does not answer another heart. His mind shrinks away if he hears only the echoes of his own thoughts and finds no other inspiration.

—Pearl S. Buck

Thirst

Anne Lamott

I knew by the time I was twenty that I was an alcoholic, even though I was not quite sure what that meant: Dylan Thomas said an alcoholic was someone you don't like who drinks as much as you do. I thought I was a good alcoholic, mostly pleasant, maybe too affectionate after a few drinks, perhaps a little loud sometimes or weepy, but not a burden to anyone except myself. I liked being an alcoholic; I liked drinking and getting high or drunk with other people like me—I thought of us as being like everyone else, only more so. More alive. Deeper. More in touch with—with what? With spirit—our own—and with spirits: of the times, of humanity . . . and all sorts of other bullshit we tell ourselves when we have lost the ability to control our drinking.

One day in 1985, I woke up so hungover that I felt pinned to the bed by centrifugal force. I was in the sleeping loft of my little houseboat in Sausalito. The sun was pouring in and the birds were singing and I was literally glued to my pillow by drool. I decided to quit drinking. And I was doing quite well, remarkably well, in fact, until five o'clock that first night. Then the panic set in. Thankfully, I had a moment of clarity in which I understood that the problem was not that I drank so much but that I drank too quickly. The problem was with *pacing*. So I had a good idea. I would limit myself to two beers a night. Two beers! What a great idea.

I went to the market, which was one block away, and got two beers—two beers, sort of. What I bought were two sixteen-ounce Rainier Ales. Now Rainier Ale is fortified—it's the beer with the merest hint of raw alcohol added. It is to beer as Night Train is to wine. Winos love it, as do people from Bolinas, which is where I learned to appreciate it. It gets you very drunk very quickly, and it's cheap. What's not to love?

Okay, maybe the taste. Not all people happen to love the taste of rye bread soaked in goat urine. I myself don't mind it.

I took the two Rainier Ales home, and I drank one. I got a little high, but it was only 5:30. And I realized I was going to have to make the second sixteen-ounce Rainier Ale last until bedtime. So after I put on my thinking cap, I realized that if I was going to pace myself successfully, I might need a little . . . supplement.

Luckily I had a Nike box full of prescription pills. I have had a number of warm personal relationships with pharmacists over the years. Also, perhaps, like many female alcoholics, tiny boundary issues. So I was warm and personal with them and they would give me speed and Valium. Anyway, I took one blue Valium that night—so little, so helpless, smaller even than a Tic Tac—and washed it down with part of the second sixteen-ounce Rainier Ale. Twenty minutes later I began to feel better, a little calmer. More whole. More like God.

Then I drank the rest of the Rainier Ale and discovered that now it was only 6:30. So I smoked a little dope and took another Valium, listened to "Layla" five times, and then had a second moment of clarity: it was wonderful to want to pace yourself, but two beers a night? I mean, let's not overreact. So I went back to the market and got a third sixteen-ounce Rainier Ale and sipped it. I had to take one more tiny blue Valium, and then a Halcion, which is a sleeping pill that they have banned in most civilized countries because of unpleasant side effects. For instance, it makes you feel like killing people.

So I was able to fall asleep that night at a nice early hour, like 7:30, and I slept like a baby and woke up twelve hours later, completely refreshed. Wow! I thought. This is fantastic: no hangover, no being glued to the pillow by drool. I felt like a million dollars.

Whenever people called that morning and asked how I was, I said I felt great, which was true, and that I was on the wagon, which I believed I was, in the reform sense of the phrase.

At five that night, I went back to the market and bought three sixteen-ounce Rainier Ales. I bounced back to my house, Mary Lou Retton–like, sipped the first ale, took the Valium, smoked a joint, drank the second ale, took another Valium, listened to "Into the Mystic" ten times, drank the third ale, took the Valium and the Halcion, and discovered two unhappy facts. One was that it was only seven o'clock. The second was that I was wide awake.

Ah, I thought, here's the problem: every so often perhaps, I may need *one* extra beer. But I am going to *sip* that darned beer. So I walked to the market, a little slowly perhaps, because I was concentrating very hard on not falling over. Because that would certainly indicate that there was a problem. But I made it to the market. I bought one more sixteen-ounce Rainier Ale, and tightrope-walked back to the houseboat, where I sipped the ale, took another Valium, listened to the Duane Allman riff in "Layla" a few more times, fell asleep, and woke up twelve hours later feeling totally great.

By the fifth day, though, after drinking the first of my sixteen-ounce Rainier Ales, I began to resent anyone's attempts to control me—even my own. And so, as an act of liberation, I bought a fifth of Bushmills Irish Whiskey and had drunk it all by dawn.

It only took me one more year to admit that I could no longer control my drinking. And finally, on July 7, 1986, I quit, and let a bunch of sober alcoholics teach me how to get sober, and stay sober.

God, they were such a pain in the ass.

Let me put it this way: I didn't love sobriety at first. I thought maybe I could find a few loopholes in the basic premise of abstinence. Maybe, I thought, after a few months of sobriety, you could successfully smoke marijuana again, or maybe every anniversary you got to have one glass of a perfectly chilled California Chardonnay.

It turned out that there were not going to be any loopholes. The people who seemed to find loopholes were showing signs of failure; for instance, they were shooting themselves in the head. Over time, two of my best sober friends, thinking they'd found loopholes, shot themselves in the head and died. This got my attention.

I was, in early sobriety, too sensitive almost to live. I was like someone with psychic tinnitus; every sound or word was amplified to the point of causing me pain. The wrong whisper could pierce me like a dog whistle. Because I had not had time to develop any real self-esteem—it had been a while since I had acted in a consistently estimable way—I found offense everywhere. For instance, early on I heard a sober person say, "Religion is for people who are afraid of hell; spirituality is for people who have been there," and all I could hear was an attack on religion, on *my* religion. I couldn't hear that the person was saying that I had already gone to the most terrifying place, to the land of obsessive self-loathing, egomania, and decay, but that now, like a battered explorer, I was bravely trying to find my way home.

I was angry for a long time. I didn't know why these annoying people wanted to help me or why they seemed to love me even though I was whiny and arrogant and defeated all at once, the classic egomaniac with an inferiority complex. I finally figured it out, although I could not have put it as well as my pre-teen son, Sam, did last night. He was watching *King Kong*, the remake with Jessica Lange, and toward the end, he said, "She loves him because she can see that he's lonely."

And that is why they loved me and helped me become one of them when I grew up. Sometimes I feel that they're like the clumsy deadpan kids in *Peanuts*, with their sayings and slogans—like Pig Pen, blinky and dense, or Linus and Schroeder. But I love to listen to them tell their stories of ruin; I'm a sucker for a good resurrection story. And I love to hear of their efforts not to see what was as plain as day. I have a doctor friend, for instance, who used to shoot up sodium pentothal in his garage and then make a run for the bedroom, where he could pass out for the night; he was convinced he had a problem with insomnia, not drugs. I have a friend who could admit he was an alcoholic but then one day had to have surgery to remove pebbles from his forehead; the tiny stones got embedded while he was smashing his face against the pavement at the end of a cocaine binge. Telling me about his operation, he said with enormous hostility, "*Now* everyone's going to think I have a drug problem."

I love these stories because they show where we began, and therefore how far we have come, from the blame and delusions of our drinking days to the gentle illusions by which we stay sober. Now we understand that the blanket really *does* protect Linus and that Schroeder really *does* play lovely music on a toy piano, because both of them keep at it. They believe.

Without Me, I'm Nothing

Bonnie Wach

When the telltale blue line showed up on the little white strip, telling me I was pregnant, I sat on the edge of the toilet seat and began crying, seriously crying—not the gushing, "Honey, I have wonderful news for you" kind of tears, but "Holy mother of god, what have I done?" tears.

I should, perhaps, have taken this as a warning sign, the loud clang-clang-clang that precedes all train wrecks. But I didn't. I figured that ambivalence—even stomach-churning, appetite-losing ambivalence—was not that weird or unusual. After all, I was thirty-eight, and I'd lived a goodly chunk of a full, unencumbered life with husband, friends, family, a house, vacations in exotic places, and a modestly successful writing career. A pinch of self-doubt (okay, maybe a huge heaping truckload) in the face of such a major change seemed, if not completely natural, at least well into the normal range.

And I figured . . . well, I really *didn't* figure, I suppose, in the same way that P. and I didn't think of it as "trying" to get pregnant, but merely as "not preventing." Instead, I flushed the evidence down the toilet and went to a job interview for a magazine writing position that I had little or no interest in, calling P. on my cell phone from the parking lot of the office building.

"It's okay, it's good. It's what we wanted, isn't it?" he asked gently, while I pressed clammy palms against hot, red cheeks and tried to fathom from the eyes staring back at me in the rearview mirror if it was, in fact, what I wanted.

Unlike what we told our friends ("We feel we need to make a major life choice every decade, whether we like it or not!"), we had come to the decision to have children much as we'd decided ten years earlier to get married: tentatively, a little tearfully, half-assedly backing down the rabbit hole with one eye to the sunlight. Each of us reassuring the other that it wouldn't be that different, me secretly thinking that if it all went wrong, I could find an escape hatch—sell the house, get a divorce, climb into the Way Back Machine, and magically return my life to the way it had been before.

Marriage, it turned out, agreed with me enormously. We were nauseatingly happy—the kind of arm-in-arm, private-joke-sharing couple you'd least want to run into on the street after your boyfriend dumped you. We moved at the same speed, he and I, from the time we got up in the morning (as late as possible) to the time we went to bed at night (after the first interview on "Letterman"); a partnership on more or less equal footing—at least as much as it could be, given that he always made more money than I did.

Then we did the thing we could not undo. And as my belly swelled past the point of no return, so did my bubble of denial. When the time came, my inner nurturer would surface, I reasoned. It wasn't called maternal "instinct" for nothing, right? I headed into the delivery room armed with this flimsy bit of faith and my trusty arsenal of perfectly timed, perfectly clever responses to life's big questions.

Was it any surprise, then, that on the third day after an unplanned C-section, when they handed me a handsome, robust, and inconsolable baby boy in the middle of the night, that my little storehouse of easy one-liners proved utterly useless? As he lay wailing in my arms, all I could think was that I hadn't given life to this creature; he had taken my life from me.

Three weeks later, I was back, lying curled once again in a hospital bed, breasts dripping uselessly while I wished to god and Allah and anyone who'd listen that just this once I could have a do-over. "Are you planning on hurting yourself or your baby?" the young ER resident asked. Stripped of glib comebacks, I could only muster the flatly delivered, "No . . . not planning on it."

The official diagnosis—postpartum depression—didn't really begin to describe the place I sank to, a place where doing ordinary daily things like brushing your teeth and putting on a bathrobe were Herculean tasks. One morning, I climbed halfway up the staircase and got sideswiped by a wave of panic that literally froze me to the railing. I don't know how long I sat there, unable to get to the top and unwilling to go back down in defeat, while the phone rang and the baby cried, until my mother arrived to rescue me.

I found myself living in my own private Idaho. My life and all the things in it—the mismatched dining room chairs, the refrigerator door plastered with years of silly photos and postcards, my car, my clothes—became impenetrable mysteries to me, as if someone had taken everything and rearranged it so that it was just a half a degree off. So when I reached for the juice pitcher or the light switch, they seemed unfamiliar and wrong.

One afternoon, on a forced march through the neighborhood with the baby, I found myself accosting a mother pushing a stroller down the street. "How do you take a shower?" I demanded. "How do you take a shower and have a baby at the same time?" And when she laughed a little nervously and said, "Don't worry. It gets easier," I almost followed her home to see exactly what she meant.

The nights were the worst. On the ones when P. and I had to go it alone, when my mom took a night off to sleep, I crawled into bed and lay awake, anticipating the inevitable wailing in the next room. The sound of a baby crying is genetically programmed to dance on its mother's very last nerve, only my very last nerve was completely shot; when he cried the effect was the emotional equivalent of two verte-brae rubbing together with no disc in between to cushion them. On those nights I lay there, skin prickling with anxiety, as in that dream where you have to take a test that you haven't studied for, or when the phone rings in the middle of the night. All I wanted to do was sleep. The one thing I couldn't do was sleep.

A blur of days and weeks took me from spring to summer, but

nothing seemed to make a dent in the terror—unseen hands that grabbed at my throat in the wee hours until I could barely breathe, waves of desperation that rose up and made me gag and sweat. P., the man who up until now had finished my sentences, was empathetic, miserable, and utterly bewildered. I caught him in moments giving me the tentative sideways glance one usually reserves for a person talking to herself on a bus, or for a large, drooling stray dog roaming the streets.

"Will I ever feel better?" I asked in our almost daily, rhetorical question-and-answer session, before he went off to work.

"Of course you will."

"What if I never love being a mom?"

"You will. And in the meantime, you just love me and I'll love the baby."

"Can you stay home from work today?" I pleaded.

"You know I can't."

"What should I do?"

"Take a walk. Get outside. Call your mom."

This last question always elicited a sigh. He simply couldn't understand this part of the equation—that having a baby had some-how robbed me of my identity. No longer a member of the working world, not part of the cabal of happy new moms who met for baby yoga and decaf lattes, I had been cast adrift and was now completely without direction or purpose—uninteresting and uninterested. "What do you like to do? What do you enjoy?" he asked me. I didn't answer. I honestly couldn't think of one thing.

My mother, with whom I'd always felt a strong biological/chem-ical bond, couldn't comprehend this self-imposed exile, either. While she knew exactly what I meant when I said that the sun in September made me feel wistful and nostalgic, in this way we were completely unrelated. She was someone who had taken to motherhood like a bear to hibernation. When my older brother was born, illness kept him in the hospital for weeks, so she couldn't hold him, nurse him, mother him. She never got over it, and by the time I came along three years later, she had hunkered down so far in her den it was as though the outside world didn't exist. We were all that mattered, and she loved us with a ferocity that made us feel both secure and apprehensive. Part of me wanted to just hand over the baby to her and say, "You do it. You be the mom." And I couldn't explain to her that her willingness to do just that made me feel even more estranged from my life, more frightened.

Even in places where I should have felt some kind of kinship—new mom's classes, support groups—I was an outsider. Happy new mothers made my flesh crawl. Trust me when I tell you that nothing can drive a depressed mom to the bottom of a shame spiral faster than a circle of blissed-out breastfeeders happily comparing burping techniques, smug and satisfied in the certainty that they are exactly where they're supposed to be, doing exactly what they're supposed to be doing. Saying that your infant feels like one of those animal leg traps, and that you're contemplating chewing off your own foot to get away from it, isn't exactly the stuff of baby circle chitchat.

Likewise, nothing can reinforce the notion that you're Joan Crawford in stained sweatpants quicker than arriving, as I did, at the first meeting of a postpartum depression support group, after weeks of working up the nerve, only to discover that I was the only one who had shown up.

This notion of strength-in-numbers, misery-loves-company is perhaps the most unfortunate myth about postpartum depression. You'd think I would have taken comfort in knowing that there were others out there like me (others whom I did, in fact, encounter in subsequent, better-attended sessions of the group). But I was so acutely ashamed of my feelings that 'fessing up to anyone who seemed even slightly better off than I did felt like standing up in a room full of pacifists and announcing I was with the NRA.

The other common misunderstanding about postpartum depression is that every woman who has it suffers from a patented list of standard symptoms. Like any form of depression, PPD is not a one-size-fits-all illness, but a potent, custom-made cocktail of hormones gone haywire, bad brain chemistry, and deep insecurities upended and exposed like a raccoon-ravaged tulip garden. Everything you've ever worried about, been afraid of, ashamed of, and ambivalent about is magnified a hundred thousand times, until it feels like you're walking around inside out, your nerves and soft mental underbelly and darkest secrets hanging out for everyone to see. That's how it was for me, anyway.

So after a few botched attempts at seeking out like-minded souls, I opted instead to lurk surreptitiously in bookstores, pushing the stroller around the pregnancy and childbirth sections, pretending to be perusing *What to Expect the First Year* but secretly eyeing *The Deepest Blue: How Women Overcome Depression*. And when I finally worked up the courage to buy it, I walked up to the counter with a stack of magazines and novels and squeezed the telltale journal in the middle, hoping the clerk wouldn't notice.

When I got home, I devoured it like a nomad in the desert who's just found a puddle around a palm tree. My spirits lifted momentarily when I identified with one or two experiences in the book. But then I read on and my hopes were dashed as the author veered off on a tangent about how badly she wanted her baby, and then another about how Prozac fixed everything. She wasn't me. She couldn't help me.

And then, when I couldn't find myself in the books, when I didn't perfectly fit into one of the sanctioned categories, I sank to an even lower low. I was such a loser I couldn't even get depression right.

I wish I could point to the one thing that turned it around for me, a miracle drug that cured me, a magic button I pushed. But of course, it wasn't one thing, just as it wasn't entirely roiling hormones that took me down. My gradual recovery, over the course of a year, was brought to you in part by therapy, in which I came to understand that an unexamined life is . . . frankly, a much easier route to take, but the payoff really sucks.

With encouragement from friends, family, and my faithful gynecologist (who else do you trust with your innermost secrets?), and some trial and error, I found the support I needed. For a while, I was seeing two shrinks four times a week—my distorted, house-of-mirrors brain reasoning that if one psychiatrist could help you, two could help you twice as fast. But I eventually settled on Dr. B., whom I liked in the beginning because she never employed the inscrutable sounding-board technique ("Uh huh . . . and how did that make you feel?") and later because her gentle poking at old wounds finally made me realize that not only had they never really healed properly, but that opening them up to the air was the only thing that would.

Following her advice that "a happy mom makes a happy baby," I found part-time child care, and then did my best to let go of the mountain of guilt that came with passing off my son to someone I deemed infinitely more competent. Having stretches of time to myself once again allowed me to start taking stock of my feelings without the constant jangling interruption of a needy infant. What I discovered, surprisingly, was that lurking behind the terror, underneath the sadness, next to the shaky sociopath who was convinced she'd never love her baby, was anger—a frothing she-wolf waiting to howl. Part of that anger was aimed at myself, at my despondence, at my inability to step up to the plate and cope, and at my body's failure to deliver the euphoria that's promised, implicitly or otherwise, to every mother at childbirth.

But the bulk of my rage was directed at the nebulous silent sisterhood—at perky parenting manuals and childbirth preparation classes where disposable vs. cloth, epidural vs. natural were presented as the biggest dilemmas a new mother faces; at moms who gleefully raced back to their jobs after ten-week maternity leaves; and at women who derailed their careers to stay home with their babies and didn't admit to resenting it. Why the hell hadn't anyone warned me? Why had no one given me the slightest inkling that the rug was going to be pulled out from under me, that I was going to get plucked from the stream where I was happily swimming with the other salmon and be dumped unceremoniously in a goldfish bowl where the only thing to do was knock my head against the glass and stare at the stupid, suffocating castle day after day? Surely, somewhere in between the story about the thirty-hour labor and the rush of transcendent joy at seeing a baby's first toothless smile, someone might have slipped in "Oh and by the way, sometimes you'll wish your life had a secret trap door."

Ironically, though, the anger and alienation ultimately worked in my favor. One afternoon in therapy I confessed, "I know I should be taking the baby to the playground, but I just . . . I just don't want to. I hate it. All those zombie mommies with their snack packs and sun cream. It's a sand-infested jail cell."

"What if you didn't go to the park?" Dr. B. asked.

I had never considered that there was an alternative. That's what mothers did. Go to the park. Push their child in a swing. Crow with approval as they slid down the slide for the umpteenth time. What if I didn't go to the park? What if? From then on, my metamorphosis from retching zombie to person who could get up, brush her teeth, and dress herself in the morning (the shower thing remained rather elusive) began in earnest.

To be fair, it was helped in no small part by Zoloft. Zoloft—nail polish for the mind, the extra layer that gets between you and your feelings, the official antidepressant (seriously!) of the U.S. Olympic Games. Never a big fan of medication (P. used to berate me for refusing to take aspirin when I had a headache), I found the numbing quality of Zoloft a blessing and a curse. While it shored me up and kept the panic at bay, it also robbed me of my tears, happy and sad, and so on that day when I came upstairs to find P. sitting in the morning sunlight giving our son a bottle, his big hand cradling the baby's downy head, I felt cheated that I had nothing tangible to show for the boulder-size lump in my chest.

My recovery was aided, too, by my newly regained ability to obtain a full night's sleep. Deep, uninterrupted sleep—the miraculous healer (see also earlier reference to Zoloft). Oh, and of course, I couldn't have done it without the cooperation of the hormones, which by the seventh or eighth month had finally started to lie down and behave.

Mostly, though, my return to the world of the successful stair-climbers was brought to you by *me*. The me I found again, once I realized that being a mother didn't mean I had to give me up. One day in October I woke up in the morning and discovered that I wasn't choking with panic or fury that P. was trotting chirpily off to work. I wasn't even thinking seriously about cashing in my frequent-flier miles. And my attention turned to other things. Small things at first. The way the baby cleaned my teeth with his fingers like a tiny dental hygienist. How he gulped and laughed as he caught the warm breath I blew gently when I lay him on the changing table. That his peach fuzz smelled like a sun-drenched morning.

When I put him in the saucer seat and he covered his ears, startled by the sound of the coffee-bean grinder, I began to catch myself smiling, even laughing. One foggy afternoon, I drove past the playground to the café where we ate madeleines and mini-bagels and watched the streetcars go by for an hour and a half. Another day we sat in the car and sang Peter, Paul, and Mary's "Going to the Zoo" song and didn't actually go to the zoo. And when he shouted, "Again, again!" after we'd already sung it five times, it didn't even bother me all that much to sing it a sixth. In these moments, I recognized the first flickers of joy at being a mom.

Here was the thing: I didn't need to be in love with the mantle of motherhood. I didn't need to buy into the whole notion of moms' groups and of joyously discussing the contents of my child's diapers. I just needed to buy into the concept of being this baby's mom. And, with the global enormity of "Motherhood: The Institution" lifted from my shoulders, being just this baby's mom became manageable. I was bite-size mom, fun-size mom.

The other thing (and most of you already knew this) is that they grow on you, the little tree frogs. They look at you with laughing eyes and gummy grins, they wrap themselves around your knees, and they bury their little drooly faces in your neck—they lodge themselves into a place so deep in your heart that nothing and no one else can reach it.

Somewhere around my son's eighteen-month mark, I stood at the door of his room and watched him in his crib singing the Barney song at the top of his lungs. When he got to "With a great big hug and a kiss from me to you," his pudgy, dimpled arms spread wide to engulf me, though he couldn't see me. It was an act of complete faith, so simple yet so grand that it took my breath away. I was no less at the receiving end of that hug than if we had still been attached by an umbilical cord.

Stepping into the room, I felt like a shadow that's found its long lost body. It had been there all along, of course, even though I couldn't see it—hovering just to the side of my feet, waiting to meet my embrace.

(Learning How to) Get Laid

Jane DeLynn

B y the early seventies, I had had affairs with only two women—my high school English teacher, and someone I lived with for a year in graduate school. This second woman and I both moved to New York after graduation, but though we were still officially "lovers," I had a desire to sleep with other women. Lots of other women, casually, easily—the same way I had, in that hippie era, slept with lots of men.

My high school and college years had been before Gay Lib, when the books I read on the subject all considered homosexuality a disease—as I did myself. Until the teacher, I had never considered acting on this desire, and afterwards I assumed I would never have sex again with a woman for the rest of my life. Or, if I did, it would be some equally furtive experience, one I would be ashamed of and couldn't tell anyone about, that would have no connection with my "real" life—which, to my mind, entailed marriage. If I could have paid a woman to sleep with me I would have, but who would that be? Had any woman at all come on to me, I would have gone home with her in a second, but no one did. It's not surprising; the books I had read talked about how men succumbed to "irresistible impulses" in dangerous places such as public bathrooms, so I tended to avoid eye contact with attractive women—what if I jumped them and got thrown out of my Seven Sisters college? In the summers I occasionally roamed Central Park, where I knew men cruised, and once or twice I hung out in the bathroom at the Metropolitan Museum: everyone knew homosexuals (but perhaps not dykes?) liked art. Once an attractive woman talked to me, but it was only to ask if I was all right.

Several times in college, driven absolutely mad by desire for a woman, I'd call my high school teacher, thereby breaking a solemn promise I had made to my shrink. Although near forty, the teacher had only slept with three women before me (two of them students), but she was now sharing an apartment with my former art teacher. Somehow, I only called when the art teacher was out of town. We'd make out a little, but I wouldn't take my clothes off. Not that that would have made much difference; we had never had oral sex. Indeed, the thought of putting my mouth on a woman "down there" seemed repugnant to me, although I put guys' cocks readily enough (albeit without much enthusiasm) into my mouth.

I was promiscuous, the way people were in the sixties, partly because everybody was; partly to demonstrate I was "normal"; and partly because, as my determination to sleep with men was largely mental, it was hard to figure out precisely whom I should or shouldn't sleep with. My reasoning went like this: if I had sex with one guy I didn't especially like, what reason would I have for not having sex with the next guy I didn't especially like? Having no real bases for discrimination, I tended to base my choices on whom I thought other women—"normal women"—would find appealing. You could say, in a weird way, that I was applying the Kantian categorical imperative to the field of sexual morality, and the great numbers of sexual encounters I forced myself to have with men I didn't like (more than half were one-night stands) has warped my sexual responses, perhaps even to this day.

In graduate school in the Midwest—a place that was somehow not as "real" as New York and in which events, therefore, did not exactly "count"—with the help of LSD and similar substances, I managed to decipher the dyke beneath my soon-to-be lover's straight facade. Except for the few visits with the teacher, I hadn't had sex with a woman in over five years. But this was real sex, overnight, with a WASP who had gone to Mount Holyoke and on whom I put my mouth "down there." Still, I refused to share an apartment with her in New York: I was not ready to settle down. I had sex with her; I had sex with guys; I even had sex with some women in my consciousness-raising group who, in good feminist fashion, decided to "experiment" with having sex with a woman. Then I heard about a movement called Gay Liberation that had come along a year or two before. Before I got married (say, when I was thirty), why not sleep with as many women as I could? Wasn't I owed it, as a kind of balance for all the men I had slept with out of a sense of duty, and to make up for the five years of tortured deprivation between high school and graduate school, when the only woman I had sexual contact with (and this in a very minor way) had been my high school teacher?

But how to do this? I had met my teacher in an English class, but I was through with school. My graduate lover had been a friend first, as were the women in the C-R group. None of these women were "out" or even considered themselves gay: to this day the teacher and her lover maintain separate bedrooms, and my graduate school lover, though she has been with women ever since I've known her, still calls herself "bisexual." I knew there were bars, but I had no idea what to do in one. My encounters with men were not, I suspected, a good model. Although I personally would not have minded if a female came up to me at a bar and, after a perfunctory sentence or two, asked me "to ball," I had a feeling this was not the way lesbians went about things.

The first time I ever saw a group of gay women was at a dance sponsored by the (horrifically named) Daughters of Bilitis, an organization formed in the fifties that I had once read about in a book. The ad for the dance was in the *Village Voice*, my sole source for all things lesbian. It took me so long to dress and apply makeup that I didn't get there before 11:00 p.m. This was not because I wore anything (I'm pretty sure) other than my customary "going out" outfit—jeans and a silk shirt—but because I was so nervous. My memory is of a loft building on Prince or Spring Street, the kind artists I knew lived in—dusty uneven stairs, mail left on the hallway floor—but when I got upstairs

I was confronted by something I had never seen in any artist's loft: *women dancing together*! The sight paralyzed me: could these normal-looking people really be lesbians? Perhaps they were feminists like the women in my C-R group, women who wanted to have sex with women less out of sexual desire than from some political conviction. After all, if they were *really* lesbians and not just some straight women pretending to be lesbians, what were they doing dancing and talking instead of jumping on top of each other and fucking like rabbits right on the floor?

At the time, and for many years after, I was drawn to conventionally attractive WASPs with long hair (much like my lover)—the kind of woman I could not be accused of sleeping with because I "could not get a man." So my eyes were drawn to a blond woman with bright blue eyes wearing a preppy white shirt. She was holding hands with a somewhat taller woman with curly dark hair, someone who looked like an Italian or Jew from Queens, someone who might have even had a nose job. Someone, that is to say, who did not seem worthy of her. I was a dark-haired Jew, but I was born in Manhattan and my hair was very fine; I considered myself to have "class" in the way this other woman did not. So I stared at the blond, hoping she would lock eyes with me and in some intuitive fashion recognize (as my high school teacher and graduate-school lover had) who and what I was, and walk over to me. Instead, she averted her eyes—the first of probably hundreds of times that women have responded (or failed to respond) to me in such fashion. (I saw her in various bars over the years, but though more than once I asked her to dance, she never would.) Immediately and instinctively, I developed what became my standard response in such situations: averting my eyes as if I had not been staring, but merely scanning the room.

A woman walked over to me. She was not attractive, and I decided I would not have sex with her. She said she was an officer of the group, asked if I was nervous (which I stupidly denied), and led me across the room to where the drinks were. I immediately gulped several glasses of terrible punch. She tried to engage me in conversation, but I was too petrified to talk, so she asked if I wanted to dance.

I followed her onto the dance floor, but I couldn't move; I was both paralyzed and confused. Was she asking me to dance because she was doing her duty as a Daughter of Bilitis, or because she wanted to have sex with me? I did not know the conventions of lesbian relationships—for all I knew, accepting an invitation to dance was code for "yes, I'll spend the night with you."

She eventually gave up on me and, excusing herself, walked over to a woman with whom she began dancing—obviously her girlfriend, for they had their arms around each other. So it was not desire but pity she had for me—an emotion I find more unpleasant than almost any other. My face burning in shame, I joined the line for the bathroom. In many a bar I have sought such refuge: the one place you can stand alone without looking pathetic.

Back then I considered myself "beautiful" in a subtle way that the average person might not notice right away, but that superior people could surely recognize. The women in the room either seemed bourgeois in a way I scorned or (even worse) appeared to be the type I soon learned to call "bridge-and-tunnel." Thinking I was more attractive than almost anyone in the room—and certainly the most intelligent and "hip"—I was surprised and annoyed that these qualities were going unnoticed. If I looked someone deep in the eyes, how could she resist me? Or, rather, if she did, surely that meant she was not worthy of me. But I also knew I had acted like a jerk, and a part of me felt I *was* a jerk. In some way I *always* felt like a jerk—from the terrible shame of wanting to have sex with women, which manifested as an overpowering self-consciousness that destroyed my ability to act like a normal human being. In this light it made perfect sense that no one wanted to talk to me. This combination of arrogance and insecurity, of feeling like both a jerk and the most desirable person in the room, accompanied me for the two-plus decades I tried to pick women up in bars—feelings that, alas, are surely not the most optimal for attracting others.

Despite my conscious lack of attraction to the lesbians in the room, I was also sure that, had any of them—even the fattest and ugliest—tailed me home and forced their way into my apartment, I

23

would have had sex with them. And—worse—enjoyed it very much.

I tried several bars after this—both the recently opened Bonnie and Clyde's and the Duchess, and the old-style establishments like Paula's, Cookie's, and Gianni's. Bonnie and Clyde's seemed the hippest, most populated with people like me, but it was Cookie's and especially Gianni's that really fascinated me. These were old-style Mafia bars filled with lesbians of the kind I had read about in now-outdated books, bars filled with butches and femmes who had been around long before Gay Lib, women who bound their breasts and passed as men, women in sexy dresses of the sort no one outside of the movies wore. Cookie's was white, but Gianni's had plenty of Latins, women who danced in an old-fashioned way, one partnering the other. Role-playing between men and women had been condemned by the feminist movement in the name of equality, and surely it was no better—if not worse—between women and women. But part of me was attracted to it, as if I were watching a fifties movie. And, as in fifties movies, I could not tell if it was the girl in the sexy dress I wanted to be, or the guy who had his arms around the girl in the sexy dress. I dressed so differently from anyone in Gianni's that I didn't take it personally that no one talked to me; these truck drivers and secretaries, construction workers and waitresses and cosmeticians (or so I imagined them to be) lived in a world unimaginably different from mine.

Then I went to a dance, sponsored by either the Gay Activist Alliance or the Gay Liberation Front, in an old SoHo firehouse soon to be destroyed by arson. The dance was coed, and the presence of the men made me feel comfortable: they were hip and good-looking, much more my type than the lesbians I had seen in bars. Always, I felt better in bars when men were around: partly because of their promiscuity, which I admired and envied; partly because it's easier to flirt with someone you don't want to sleep with; and partly because, in some sense, I felt that in relation to women—especially in my attitude toward sex with women—I *was* a man.

For the first time in a gay venue, I was asked to dance. A man asked me, so I wasn't nervous. When I'm not nervous, I dance fairly well, and when the song ended and the man left, a woman came over to me. She wore a man's white T-shirt and had her hair cut almost in a crewcut. This was way before punk, a time when even men still had long hair, so to my mind this made her very butch, even though she was rather small and delicate. To dance with someone like that in Gianni's was one thing, but in a brightly lit room in SoHo where it was not impossible I might run into some gay guy I knew. . . . On the other hand, my feminist principles told me I should dance with any-one who asked: I hated the cliquishness of dyke bars, the rather high school way certain people were "in" or "out." So I started to dance with her, in the clunky, separate way one did then, but she touched my arm, and the touch of her arm set my skin on fire, and I let her pull me to her. My pants grew wet, but when the song ended I walked away: she was so clearly a person I could not be seen with.

"Carrie" (as I'll call her) came over with a drink for me, but I soon left her to cruise the room. She watched me as, emboldened, I asked a woman to dance, a woman I had noticed watching me as I danced with Carrie, a woman who (I therefore thought) must be attracted to me. But the woman refused, and looked at me with what seemed like disdain. I assumed the disdain was due to my dancing with someone who looked so butch, and I decided that, utopian motives aside, it was not socially productive to dance with anyone who asked.

My chances for the evening apparently ruined, I decided to go home. I gave Carrie a slight nod, which she must have interpreted as apology for my rejections, for she came over and asked if she could come with me. I told her no, but she followed me out the door. This was annoying; the last thing I wanted was for anyone to think I was going home with her. But she took my anger in good humor, and began walking with me.

How it came to pass that I agreed to spend the night with her, I don't remember; perhaps she touched my arm again. Some people are like that—repugnant though you may find them, the slightest touch sets you aflame. I made her promise to walk behind me to my house and to pretend she wasn't with me if we ran into someone I knew.

Why Carrie put up with this I don't know, but she did. And yes, she made me burn. She telephoned several times, but I refused to make a date with her. Then one night I ran into her at Bonnie and Clyde's, and somehow she ended up coming home with me. (Again, I made her walk behind me.) On the way up the stairs to my Bowery loft, we ran into my neighbor, and I found myself making up some lame explanation for who Carrie was and why I was with her. I was angry at her for putting me in this spot, but the touch of her arm . . .

As I refused to be seen in public with her, Carrie and I never went out on a formal date. But from time to time I'd let her visit me, or she'd just come by and ring my bell. She worked in a T-shirt factory, and one night she brought me a present: a dark blue T-shirt with hammered metal dots in the shape of a Jewish star.

I was embarrassed by the T-shirt and wouldn't wear it. But in retrospect it touches me, this gift from my blue-collar lesbian. As time passed, my cruising improved, but it was never very good. Despite endless efforts (and despite being a writer), I never managed to come up with a good pickup line, and I usually had to get drunk to approach someone. More than once I lurched from the Duchess to the Cubbyhole and back again (or even to the Cubbyhole and back *again*). Pathetic.

Even so, over the years I managed to go home with quite a number of women. Credit this to persistence. Each conquest boosted my confidence, and time taught me some things: anyone at the bar past 2:30 A.M. *really* wants to get laid. Many, if not most, of the women I had sex with just once, but I still have fond memories of them: they were people who, if I didn't connect with on a sexual level, I wouldn't have connected with at all.

In 1991, I was in Saudi Arabia, reporting on the first Gulf War. More than once I had to take refuge in some shelter when Scuds were coming my way. I was nervous, of course, but not nearly as nervous as I'd been in any number of dyke bars, wondering what kind of luck might come my way that evening.

Writing for the Cure

Elizabeth Fishel

"Nine doors will close in your face," my father often told me, "before the tenth one opens." My father was a long-time ad man with a poet's soul and an ace reporter's nose for the story. He had spent his working life knocking on doors that swung open and closed, closed and open, selling people products they didn't know they wanted and arguably didn't need. An optimist with a pessimist's history, he had always managed to get to yes even after a maddening battery of no's. And retiring, he'd turned his expertise pro bono, lining up lucrative ads for an award-winning newspaper written and run by New York inner-city youth.

As I hit mid-life with the new millennium, my ears buzzed with the harsh finality of slamming doors. My mother died after a long, grueling battle with breast cancer. My older son got ready to leave home for college three thousand miles away. My latest book came out, the one into which I'd poured four years of work and for which I had four years of high hopes; despite good reviews, it did not exactly fulfill my fantasies of best-sellerdom and early retirement. Staring at those closed doors—those relationships over or morphing into who-knew-where, those projects stymied—I felt no-exit stuck. Night after night, I'd wake into the unforgiving glare of 3:00 A.M., restless with hormones and self-doubt, and toss and turn until dawn. "Necessity is the reinvention of mother," was an essay I started to write but, no surprise, could never quite finish. I dreamed of reinvention, I hungered for it, but I didn't know where to begin.

Still, once a week, I put my own stalled plans aside to guide a group of women writers along their literary journey, to nurture their dreams. Like a therapist who struggles with personal demons but who still keeps appointments with patients, I showed up. For ten years, I'd been meeting every Wednesday morning with these twelve or so women of all ages and life-stages—from twenty-something to seventy-plus but mostly at life's midpoint like myself—who gathered in my living room to hone their craft. Part writing class, part support group, part literary salon, our writers' community had a core of members who had stayed for the long haul, while others came for a session or two and moved on, making room for new blood. In other worlds they were doctors and lawyers, therapists and publicists, mothers taking time out from child-raising to probe their own thoughts, claim their own voices. Sinking comfortably into sofa and armchairs, sipping strong coffee or peppermint tea, they and I aired and shared dreams and doubts, and learned what it meant to write from the heart. We'd stuck together through marriages and divorces, babies and grandbabies, career shifts and retirement, illness and recovery, transforming our "diamonds in the dustheap"—in Virginia Woolf's famous phrase—into all varieties of first-person writing.

Our meetings provided a welcome breather for me from the isolation of creative work and the computer screen's stern stare. The group's positive energy—and that Wednesday deadline—did wonders for everyone's productivity, including mine.

Most of the women were unpublished when they joined the group, writing first for pleasure and self-revelation. I preached the joys of process over product and stressed the sloppy first draft. The difference between published and unpublished, I promised, was fanny-on-chair perseverance. I told them to strap themselves to their desk chairs by the sash of their bathrobes, if necessary, as John McPhee once confessed that he did. Then I pushed them to polish draft after draft until they shone. "No writer gets it right the first time" became our group's mantra.

One by one the writers who were ready started sending out their work for publication. I dusted off my father's words of wisdom. "Nine doors will close in your face," I told them, braced for those inevitable first rejections, standing by with Kleenex—and extra mailing envelopes. Then, gradually, as I knew it would, that tenth door started creaking open for a few of them. One writer entered a local book-store's annual travel-writing contest and won first prize, a plane ticket to anywhere in the world. A few started appearing on the op-ed pages of local newspapers with pieces on the Mideast conflict, the roots of terrorism, and other global hot buttons. And two women who'd never published a word pitched a column idea to their suburban paper and got the job—a bimonthly column they wrote together called "Double Talk." Those first bylines inspired us all.

Occasionally we'd fantasize about publishing a collection of our work, but when I sent a prototype to my agent, a copy of the annual anthology we produced ourselves, she dismissed it. Anthologies don't sell, she cautioned, and anthologies by unknown writers . . . forget it.

Little did I imagine that helping midwife these fellow writers' dreams would help me get back my own. For we were all, all of us Wednesday writers, women on the cusp, women in transition. Almost all were drawn to the group to make sense of life passages and upheavals, to use the steady, unflinching gaze of introspection to reveal resilience. We were all mining our inner lives, first to under-stand ourselves better, then to reach out and resonate with others. "The personal life deeply lived," wrote Anaïs Nin, "goes beyond the personal." We wrote for our own survival and to prove this larger mis-sion true.

Rebecca was a new mother who had inadvertently let her tiny baby slip out of her arms onto the sidewalk; the baby survived the accident, but Rebecca was thrown into a tailspin of guilt and recrimi-nation. Writing her soul-baring essay, "Cradle and All," she confronted the myth of the perfect mother and finally forgave her-self—and reader-mothers everywhere—for simply being good enough. Diana's oldest daughter was gearing up for high school in another town, and Diana was dissolving in tears, even cornering her bank teller to commiserate. In "Letting Go," she began to move beyond sorrow until she could watch her daughter's leap of growth with pleasure and pride. Kathleen and Joan, both active and in great shape, each suffered scary heart episodes that landed them in the hospital. Their column, "The Heart of the Matter," recounted the swift interventions that saved their lives, and they won an American Heart Association award for alerting other women to potential heart health dangers.

Meanwhile the shadow of breast cancer darkened our close-knit circle, mirroring the national epidemic. Mothers, sisters, friends and a sobering handful of the Wednesday writers themselves coped with it, wrote about it, and did their best to carry on. In "After Paris," Liz recalled the sensuous pleasures of a trip to France before returning to a cancer diagnosis and a long ordeal of treatment, ultimately successful. But two group members were not so lucky. During the ten years we had been meeting, twice the group went together to memorial services for writers whose lives had been cut short by cancer.

Then my mother died. Watching her valiant three-year struggle against this relentless opponent filled me with roiling emotions that matched the complexities of our relationship—admiration, sadness, fear, powerlessness. After she died I felt so hollow and removed, I understood why mourning women in other cultures cloaked themselves in black robes. It was protective armor: "Don't come too close or expect too much of me," it announced. For weeks after her death, the only writing I did was answering condolence notes and confiding to my journal as I tried to make sense of my mother's life and her loss.

But eventually, after months of mourning, I knew it was time to transform my grief into something positive. My mother had been a doer, a talented multi-tasker—professional ceramicist, avid tennis player, financial whiz, ardent traveler. Her letters, full of family news and mother-wisdom, were characteristically signed not "Love" or "Yours," but "Rushing." She also knew how to worry a problem until a solution emerged. My mother's daughter—and in her honor—I knew I needed a course of action, some way to make a difference for other breast cancer patients, some means of raising money to combat this disease that took too many precious lives. Inspiration came quickly, spawned as I mused about the fundraising marathons that bring money and attention to a variety of worthy causes. For several years, my mailbox had overflowed with requests from friends putting their bodies on the line for heart disease, leukemia, ALS. But since I didn't run or bike or even walk huge distances, I wanted to use the one skill I could sustain for long periods of time—writing. Not logging miles but spinning words would be my contribution.

If necessary, I was prepared to tackle the project alone. But as soon as I broached the subject, my sympathetic sorority of writers rallied to the cause. We mobilized quickly with a two-step fundraising plan. Our beneficiary, we decided after much brainstorming, would be the Carol Franc Buck Breast Care Center at the University of California, San Francisco, a state-of-the-art treatment and research center in our Bay Area community and a model nationwide. We planned a day-long literary event at the University, "Healing Words," that would feature readings by acclaimed writers, headlined by Rachel Naomi Remen, as well as breast cancer survivors sharing their own experiences. There we would launch an anthology of our writing and continue to sell it with all proceeds donated to the Breast Care Center. Welcome seed money came from the hospital's auxiliary, which believed in our project when it was just a gleam in our eye.

To short-circuit the hunt for a publisher and build on our momentum, we decided to take on the publishing process ourselves. I had published four books the traditional way, and each had dallied at least a year in production. But never underestimate a group of writers in high gear. Our womanpower, combined with the high-tech advantages of our digital age, produced our book in just five months.

Collective energy plus tenacity and ingenuity fueled the project from the get-go. We started by e-mailing all the writers who'd been in the group for the past ten years—about fifty—and gave each of them the chance to submit one or two of her first-person essays. Thirty-two writers responded, and my coeditor Terri Hinte (in real life publicity director for a local record company) and I chose the best of their best for the book. We also included pieces by the two members who had died—and dedicated the book to their memory. The resulting anthology—*Wednesday Writers: Ten Years of Writing Women's Lives*—was a poignant collection of work on family and identity, love and loss, illness and recovery, and the daily pleasures and surprises of ordinary life. I saw now how well the group had succeeded in its goal and appreciated its gift: to write passionately about the personal life deeply lived. Touching universal themes, each of us had written from the emotional center and reached for the reader's heart. What emerged was a portrait of contemporary women that was resonant, complex, and well rounded.

Although only a few of the essays centered on illness, we kept in mind the reason for the book's existence as we organized the pieces thematically into sections, among them "Pleasures," "Family Tales," "Transitions," and "Healing Words." This last in particular reflected our shared dedication to the recuperative power of writing through loss, grief, and crisis. "After my cancer diagnosis I believe it was writing as much as medical treatment that enabled me to heal," explained one of the Wednesday writers, voicing the anthology's take-away message.

Engrossed in our project, busy and engaged, I too was gradually beginning to heal from my midlife malaise. The details of organizing and editing the manuscript were starting to eclipse the creative doubts that had stopped me in my tracks, and the company of thirty other women captivated me more than navel gazing. When I woke in the middle of the night, I'd count our contributors or pieces still left to edit instead of numbering my own flaws and failings. Soon, I stopped waking altogether, and my days revved up with renewed energy.

In a couple of months, Terri and I had edited, organized, and digitally formatted the book. For its jacket, we chose the eye-catching image of a woman's uplifted torso by another group member, Mary Jo Murphy. This nude had graced every cover of the annual class anthology we'd produced ourselves since we'd first been meeting. But over ten years, some things had changed. Mary Jo generously updated the

torso's curves to reflect our decade of expanding middle-aged ampli-
tude.

Cover-to-cover ready, the book was then dispatched to a local
printer. A month later, the first copies appeared—alas, riddled with
errors. They had been produced from an old, uncorrected, digital
file—entirely not our fault—and were redone, gratis, just in time for
our first "Healing Words" fundraiser. No first edition was ever more
cherished, no longed-for baby more coddled by its thirty-plus god-
mothers.

Wednesday Writers benefited from the group's energy at every
stage of the publishing process, but most especially in launching and
promoting the book. As an author, I know how vital it is to activate
one's network of friends, family, and acquaintances to put out the
word about a new book; in our case we had thirty-two dedicated
women activating thirty-two networks. And every one of us brought
something to the party. Collectively, we sent out company-wide pro-
motional e-mails; bought the book in bulk for family and friends; sold
it at children's school fairs, trunk sales, and alumni gatherings; even
posed with it on holiday photo cards; and gave it as hostess gifts—at
twelve dollars, it was no more expensive and far longer lasting than a
bottle of wine.

The combination of passionate personal writing by a group of
ordinary women, most never before published, and the book's goal as
a fundraiser for breast cancer research touched a nerve in Northern
California with ripples nationwide. A month after publication, for
two weeks running, *Wednesday Writers* appeared on the *San Francisco
Chronicle's* Bay Area paperback best-seller list, galloping right behind
Seabiscuit. Terrific media attention followed, with features and glowing write-ups in a multitude of local publications. Spring, summer,
fall, we were booked solid with readings and events, a heady fifteen
minutes of fame for all of us. As of this writing, we've gone into three
printings and books are still selling briskly.

Celebrating the anthology's first anniversary, we've contributed
more than twelve thousand dollars to the Breast Care Center. Now
we joke that we, like the British "Calendar Girls," are women of "a

certain age" who've raised money and attention for our cause. But we did it without even taking off our clothes.

So while I'd been knocking on nine other doors, *Wednesday Writers* proved to be the tenth. The camaraderie and shared pleasures of our collaborative effort energized me out of my midlife doldrums, and contributing to an important cause gave me a sense of larger purpose and focus; in contrast, my own problems downsized to a manageable scale. Professionally, I reaped the benefits of the book's positive trickle-down. Our many public appearances and media coverage brought the group welcome attention, and new writers clamored to join. The Wednesday morning meetings grew so crowded that I started a Friday session as well. Invitations to do readings and give talks got me back in circulation, revitalized and with a new subject I felt passionate about. My writers' groups had become an intimate community, and guiding them anchored and inspired my creative life.

As for my abandoned essay on reinvention? I managed to finish it just in time to include it in *Wednesday Writers*. This time a door had barely closed before I could hear it swinging open again to let in the fresh breeze of something new.

One Is Silver and the Other Gold

Nancy Wartik

After a several-year hiatus, I've recently begun to date again. Nothing's changed much about dating since I last did it: the best places to connect are still at parties, online, and through acquaintances. When I meet someone, I still analyze the subtext of casual chat to see if we're compatible. Still hope I don't exude that telltale air of desperation, which might drive someone away. Still fret, after a first date, over whether there's chemistry and if so, who should call whom. Once or twice, when my follow-up calls haven't been returned, I've been left to wonder anxiously what went wrong: something I said, something I did?

Since I've been doing this for nearly a year, I've had a few bona fide relationships, though one I had some hopes for crashed and burned. But I know that in the dating arena, the usual sports clichés apply: you've got to jump back in that saddle! Winners never quit and quitters never win! So I do my best to get out there and try, try again. At least this time I can go to my husband for consolation. Because one other thing is different about dating these days: I'm not looking for romance but for moms—specifically for moms with whom to be friends.

By that, I don't just mean discussing children's sleep schedules, or how many Elmo videos they should watch a day, or how to get a finicky eater to chow down. It's not that I'm not grateful for moms with whom to share that kind of exchange; definitely, I am. But ultimately, I'm looking for relationships that define themselves by more than the common denominator of parenting, for the thick-and-thin kind of friendships I made before I took on the matron role. Our daughter, Mira, was eleven months old when my husband and I adopted her and brought her home to New York City from Kazakhstan. A year later, among the multitude of changes motherhood has made in my life, one of those I've struggled with most involves my friendships. I haven't found parenting and friendship to be a simple, easy fit. Becoming a mother has altered the dynamics of some longstanding relationships, while pushing me into a search for kindred spirits at a time in my life when I don't know if I can still make the intimate connections that happen more easily when you're fresher, less set in your ways, and don't feel like a ninety-year-old by the end of each day.

Yet those are the sorts of connections I'm hoping to find. I have high standards based on years of experience. And I'm too old and crotchety now to be satisfied with less.

As I write this, I've been married for two years and nine months, which hardly qualifies me as a newlywed. Even so, by my own scientific calculations, I've spent 94.4% of my life single. (The mathematically minded can amuse themselves by inserting this data into an algebra equation that will yield my current age.) During the years when I was on my own, I had my share of relationships, but it was my friendships that sustained me over the long haul. Friends were the people I called to whine to at one o'clock in the morning during endless dry romantic spells, when I was sure I'd never have sex again. They were the people with whom I traveled, bickering on the island of St. John and then celebrating after surviving a first scuba dive; to whose care I relinquished myself while prostrate with the worst migraine of my life in a remote Guatemalan hotel room at 3:00 A.M., unable to swallow so much as an aspirin because there was no potable water. They were the people who put up with my moodiness, eccentricities and neuroses, and loved me anyhow. We worked through problems together—or didn't. There are lost friendships I've mourned as much as any romantic relationship that didn't work out.

Since birds of a feather flock together (to switch from sports clichés to ornithological ones), many of my closest companions were single like me. We were women in our thirties and forties walking a similar path. We spoke a certain, comfortable shorthand because we knew each others' lives—what was good, what was hard about them. When to offer comfort or encouragement or indignation (invariably over some oafish male behavior). When it was best to say nothing at all.

Then, one night, at a New York City gallery opening, I met a man, fell in love, and after a couple of years, I married him. I was well aware that by the standards of our day, I'd pulled off a slight miracle, meeting the right person in the urban jungle when I was already a geriatric case (i.e., over forty). But I wrestled at times with an unwelcome sense that I was heading down a road that branched off from the one my uncoupled comrades were traveling. The hardest point for me came one New Year's, when a group of my women friends went to Italy together. My husband-to-be couldn't go, and so I didn't either. But not going made me feel torn up inside. I hated knowing they were there and I wasn't—I felt excluded from a club to which I hadn't even realized my allegiance. The fact that I'd excluded myself voluntarily was little consolation.

If getting married gave me the feeling that my road had diverged in certain ways from some of my friends, now that I'm a mother, I sometimes feel like I've thumbed a ride and am whizzing off down that road in a Maserati. It's not just that my time is so compromised, or my freedom radically constrained. Parenthood has shifted my perspective more dramatically than anything else in my life ever has. The thing I've come to care most about in the last year—being a good mother to my daughter—isn't part of some of my closest friends' immediate experience. We can't always speak the same kind of shorthand now.

Occasionally, small things bring this home. Once, a friend e-mailed a last minute suggestion that a group of us go to dinner and mentioned that we were welcome to bring Mira. It was obviously a well-meaning comment, but to my ears, it rang as if she'd said, "You're welcome to bring your left arm with you." It hadn't occurred to me to ask if Mira could come, because you don't ask if you can bring part of yourself when you go out. Moreover, making dinner plans as a parent rarely involves just a casual decision to bring or not bring the baby. Our daughter, in particular, is a terror in restaurants; adult conversation is impossible if you're chasing a toddler around and through the legs of understandably nonplussed waiters. But to corral a sitter on short notice can give pause to even the stoutest heart. (Not to mention that unless you're independently wealthy, including a sitter in your plans sets a meter running in your head all night, ticking off the increasingly larger small fortune you owe.) My friend's innocent comment hit me like a tiny epiphany, a revelation that the childless and the child-ed often inhabit different worlds, whether or not they want it to be so.

Certainly, I didn't take other people's parenting concerns into account when I lived child-free. Why should I have? There's no reason, if you're not a parent, to consider the going rate for sitters, or the thought process that goes into packing up a baby for long-distance transport (i.e., two blocks). Nor did I always welcome friends including children in our plans, to begin with. Children are an ongoing distraction; their presence can't help but change the texture and content of a social occasion. Yet once or twice, when it's been hinted it might be nice if we hired a sitter rather than show up with Mira, I've felt myself grow huffy. Who *wouldn't* want the rare treat of being around our incomparable daughter for an evening? Never mind that a few years ago, the person not wanting it might have been me. For better, for worse—and I really don't always know which—that's not who I am anymore.

There are more subterranean currents I've feared might carry me away from some of the people I love. Having undertaken marriage and motherhood at an age when some women are already grandmothers, I'm well acquainted with the wrenching struggle many childless women in midlife go through over the "baby thing."

I experienced it in spades, myself. And while it's fine in theory to say we should want only the best for those we care about, should revel in their triumphs and take joy in their happiness . . . well, personally I've always thought a little pinch of schadenfreude is a delightful way to start each new day. When I was single and friends announced they were having a baby—and more so the older I got—I wanted to slit my wrists, trip an old lady in the street, or both. I gave baby presents and made admiring noises over the new offspring. Sometimes I grew to love those offspring in spite of myself. But unmixed joy was hardly an accurate description for what I felt about the concept of other people's children.

And when we adopted Mira? One of my best friends and I, after some painful silences and wilted attempts, managed to steer through the conversational minefield of what it means for me to have a child, while she's started to brood about her options closing on that front. She admitted she found it grating to listen to me complain about the hardships of parenthood while she was grappling with anxiety over whether it would even happen for her.

Another of my best friends and I, after ongoing tension that flared once or twice into argument, have talked fairly openly about seeing our relationship through the choppy waters of my changed status. I'd been short-tempered and snappish in the weeks after bringing Mira home, my friend said (okay, there might be a tiny bit of truth to the claim) and she hadn't always known how to approach me. I'm grateful—very grateful—for these exchanges, which weren't always easy but ultimately cleared the air. I worry, though, about other conversations not yet had, perhaps never to be had, with other friends still trying to make their peace with the "baby thing," or with whom talk flows less easily. I can only conjecture what might be in their minds. I don't know if my conjectures are right. If so, though, I understand the feelings all too well.

Maybe another reason I've been keenly aware of my friendships this year is that after getting home and spending, oh say, about fifteen minutes alone with our adorable new daughter, I was ready to check into the nearest insane asylum. I chose and still choose to be a part-time stay-at-home parent. But after we got back from Kazakhstan, after a wonderful welcome party and nonstop visits from well-wishers, after my parents left town and my husband went back to work and it was just Mira and me, I realized I hadn't the faintest idea what you do with a baby all day long. You can't chat with it, or go to the movies; you certainly can't get any work done. Instead, your hours revolve around fun pursuits like wiping up half-chewed food that's been hurled onto the floor or grabbing the baby up when she's lying on the cat and squishing it. It turns out, I don't *like* playing with wooden cutout puzzles or plastic stacking cups; in fact, generally speaking, I suck at baby games. If this was life with a child, how was I ever going to survive each day, each hour, each minute? And why wasn't I in a transport of maternal bliss, after craving this for so long?

One day in desperation I called a friend, whose son is about Mira's age, at her office. Getting right to the point, I told her I was ready to shoot myself. Why was I so miserable and confused when I clearly knew I should be happy and grateful? A couple of days later she came over to spend an afternoon with us. She wasn't remotely surprised at how I was feeling. "I'd rather have a job pushing rocks up a hill all day than spend each day being a mother," she told me. When she did have to do mom time, she depended on the kindness of strangers: she'd taken to collaring people pushing strollers in her neighborhood or on the subway, and soliciting them as possible friends. To make it out of parenthood alive, she needed the company of others in her same boat—people to whom she could speak in short-hand.

And so began my hunt for matched sets of pals: baby friends for Mira, mom friends for me. Early on, I was approached by a neighbor whose child is near Mira's age and we hopefully set up a couple of play dates. Our kids got along but we couldn't locate the sense of simpatico between us. By unspoken mutual agreement, no further play dates were proposed. I met another mom at a party, a pretty, young teacher who liked how our daughters interacted. We had a play date and talked about possibly sharing a sitter. I thought I saw friendship potential after another play date and suggested a third get-together. I never heard back. I ran down a laundry list of possibilities: I was too old for her, too odd; perhaps she disapproved of my parenting style. (Hadn't she heard the classic three date rule—you always give someone three chances before you dump them?) It was about then that I saw I really was in the dating world again, with all its concomitant angst, ego blows, and neurotic-making encounters.

Sometime in late spring, not so long after we'd brought Mira home and while I was still shell-shocked at the realities of parenting, I met another neighborhood mother. We seemed to have much in common—both of us were "older" and worked in a similar field. We were interested in books, movies, politics, and relationships, and didn't confine ourselves to talking mostly about children. When we met for play dates, I invariably enjoyed our conversations. I wondered if this might be the kind of mom I'd been looking for, a person I'd gravitate to whether or not we had kids. But tension began to build between us over problems related to a parenting issue, the sordid details of which I'll spare you. I was irked and it probably showed. Our friendship began to wither on the vine and today, when we see each other in the neighborhood, we barely speak. I'm not sure if our friendship would have failed its first test under any circumstances, or whether something about the peculiar intensity or complexity of parenting concerns did us in. Either way, it hurt, briefly. But that's the dating life.

Hoping to meet other mothers, I joined a "mommy and me" gym class with my agile, energetic daughter, but found myself almost the lone mom among a cluster of nannies. Meanwhile, as any serious dater does these days, I'd also turned to the Internet. On a message board for New York moms I found a play group forming near me. I was one of the first to join and soon we were a revolving group of about ten women meeting weekly, toddlers in tow. For the past year, this group has given Mira and me something to look forward to each week; it's also been a font of information about parenting strategies. What I don't yet know is whether, when the group scatters, I'll have made lifelong pals. Perhaps it's the nature of the group situation, perhaps the geriatric mom thing again (I could be, if not a mother to many in the group, at least their aged aunt). Perhaps it's simply a difference in sensibilities. Whatever the reason, I haven't fallen into conversations that stray far from the topic of the children themselves—a wonderful topic, a worthy topic, but not one that a friendship can sustain itself on indefinitely.

It may be shortsighted, though, to ask the group to be other than it is. On at least one occasion already, it's saved my sanity. This past winter, Mira and I were sick with bronchitis that she'd caught from me or I from her. For several days, we'd barely left the house and I was starting to lose my grip. The group was meeting at my home that week and I e-mailed to warn the others that there would be a miniature germ factory in their midst. I said I'd understand if they didn't want to come. But those who were available showed up, and while Mira dozed in my lap, the other kids played. I was so appreciative they'd risked life, limb, and exposure to bronchitis in order to stop by, it practically made me teary-eyed.

Looking at where things stand now, even I, armed with my trusty philosophy that it's always best to look on the dark side, can see light on the horizon. When I became a parent, my mother suggested that eventually I'd find myself socializing only with other parents because anything else would be too inconvenient. At the time it seemed preposterous; I vowed it would never happen. Today, I better understand what she meant but plan to stick with my original vow. Recently, one of the friends I've occasionally clashed with over my new, baby-owning status, told me she's noticed and appreciates how hard I've worked to stay in touch with her lately, during a period when she's been going through her own ups and downs. Not to pat myself on the back—that would be far too psychologically healthy a gesture—but that acknowledgment meant a lot to me.

I've also started to feel more measured, less desperate, about the maternal dating game. It helps that after a year, I understand this business of parenting a little better; it helps that I've come to love my daughter so much that I sometimes forget what's hard about staying home with her and only remember how incredibly lucky I am. What's more, after my first disappointing stab at making a close mom friend, I've found there are other fish in the sea (to finish up with a jaunty, nautical cliché). I've met a neighborhood mom whose company I enjoy apart from the time spent prying our screaming daughters' fingers apart as they fight for possession of a stuffed hedgehog. I look forward to our play-date sessions as a distraction not only for Mira but for me as well.

Perhaps in a year of such cataclysmic change, it sounds trivial to admit that making and keeping friendships has ranked so high on my "to worry" list. God knows it's a lengthy list, crammed with the kinds of things most trendy new moms worry about these days. I've felt guilty that I don't spend enough time with Mira, guilty that I don't spend enough time working. I've fretted over whether you can still call yourself a feminist if, most nights, you're to be found in the kitchen making dinner, with a Sesame Street video braying in the background, while you wait for your hubby to come home from the office. I've watched with chagrin as the image I had of myself as an effortlessly patient and loving parent shattered into a million little pieces the moment I actually became a mother. Don't such concerns somehow have a heftier ring to them than do my anxieties whether I've got enough buds right now?

It might seem that way, of course, because the world hasn't typically given much weight to women's relationships with each other—but I'll forego the feminist rant. The reality is, friendships have always loomed large in my own psychic landscape and have given an abundance of meaning to my life. As my daughter grows up, I want her to know what it's like to have close friendships, I want her to be able to see them as part of the fabric of our family life. I suppose the measure of my success will be some years from now, when Mira begins seeking refuge from her impossible, embarrassing parents, in the bosom of her own close group of friends.

The Lioness Sleeps Tonight

Jane Ganahl

I lunched the other day with Xandra, a girlfriend I had not seen much of these last ten years, since we stopped working in the same office. Ours is one of those friendships that exists on the periphery of life: the kind that doesn't require daily or even monthly calls, the kind that leaves your personal space uninvaded—but that, every so often, you make time for. And you're always glad when you do, because your bond is such that it feels like no time has passed.

Sitting across the table from Xandra at a seafood dive, I was taken by how great she looked. Devoutly anti–plastic surgery, she was starting to show all fifty-five of her years, but had the torque and stride of a woman to be reckoned with, and the body that comes with being a gym Nazi one's whole life. (Note to self: in next life, make working out as much of a priority as family, friends, fun, work . . . and *food*.)

She drove herself as hard as she did everyone around her—one reason her relationship history had been sketchy. Two marriages, several broken engagements. She was a classic tough, no-bullshit broad, and didn't suffer foolish men gladly, which meant that she sometimes paid for her standards by being alone. Then again, I thought, she was rarely unhappy.

Xandra told me about a friend of hers I hadn't met. This woman, fifty like me, had spent a spectacular weekend with an even more spectacular man—possibly the One of her Dreams. They went to Carmel to antique-shop and wound up checking into the Highlands Inn, where they could not keep their hands off each other for three days. Then, as they were saying goodbye on Sunday evening, he told her that he just wasn't interested in seeing her again. He said there wasn't enough chemistry to sustain them.

"Can you imagine?" Xandra exclaimed, eyebrows arched. "My friend was flabbergasted! She is so used to getting every guy she wants, she just could not believe that he was passing her up!"

She paused and looked straight into my eyes. "The only other woman I know with that kind of chutzpah is you."

Me? The idea was so startling I dropped my forkful of calamari *fritti*. "Me?" I laughed. "Xandra, I don't think I ever had that kind of chutzpah."

"You most certainly did!" she said indignantly. "During the years that we covered City Hall you left a trail of broken hearts. Remember Stuart? Pete? And that young NPR radio intern? There were so many. You were such a hunter—a real lioness. You saw a guy you liked and you went after him. They were meat!"

I blushed, taking guilty pleasure in the characterization of myself as a man-eater. "Yes, I suppose it was like that once," I sighed, sounding more like my late granny than someone with a few milli-liters of hormones left in her body. "But it hasn't been like that since . . . "

"Since *when*?" Xandra challenged.

Since . . . I had to really think about it. When I survey my last decade, I see that there has definitely been a slowing down of the parade of men through my life. I used to take secret pride in the way I commanded attention. I had friends who were much more attractive than I was, but who had half the affairs I did. There were famous men, powerful men, many men. I don't know what I had, but it was like catnip—lion-nip?—to the lads. I was fearless and horny, and utterly convinced of my own adorableness. Perhaps it was no more complicated than that.

But that was before the parade was canceled for lack of interest.

What once was like Thanksgiving Day in front of Macy's New York is now like Veterans' Day here in Half Moon Bay: a few old geezers and no brass instruments.

At the same time, there has been a slow slipping away of my confidence, my animal instincts, when it comes to the opposite sex. The lioness tiptoed back into the jungle so quietly, I barely noticed. Still, there are times when it becomes painfully clear.

Sometimes, when I catch a man's eye at a gas station, or a coffee bar, then look back at him, I'm startled if he's still staring. Not because of his audacity, but because someone finds me attractive enough to let his gaze linger. I skip the sections in department stores aimed at young wenches, knowing my body is not up to the disguise. I don't look in mirrors nearly as much as I used to, and when I have Pearl Jam or Audioslave turned up loud on my car stereo, I close the windows so no one will think I'm an old bag trying to stay young.

Nowadays, it seems, when I roar, I do it in private. If at all.

But which came first, egg or chicken? Was my self-esteem put in the crapper by a lack of male attention? Or did men stop courting me because I wasn't holding myself out as vibrant and sexy? It's a vicious cycle: men start looking past you as you age, so you start letting yourself go a bit. The health club membership falls into disuse, and Newman's Own popcorn with butter is so much better than the virtuous, unembellished kind when you have a quiet evening at home. Alone. Pass the comfort food.

It wasn't just me. Several of my friends who are my age have echoed these very sentiments. "What's the point of flirting and trying to connect if men are only interested in hooking up with women in their twenties?" one asked. "I'm in semi-retirement, dating-wise."

And that's a bit of a tragedy, because she is brilliant and lovely and successful—a fine mate for a good man. But then, one could say that of many of my peers. Yet only the hardest-headed among us—the Xandras of the world—can shrug off the slings and arrows of aging before they pierce our sense of self-worth.

It's also a classic case of use it or lose it. You stop seducing, and before too long you can't remember how to do it. Worse, you forget what the big whoop was all about. Somewhere along the line, I just stopped trying. It's like that silly (but obviously effective, since I'm remembering it) TV ad for a health club that featured a woman going to a party—with a lioness superimposed in her chest, growling as she vamps. "This is how you feel when you work out!" the voice-over proclaimed. And what happens when you don't work out? The lioness shrinks to a kitten. Or disappears.

I'd met someone just a few weeks earlier, at a music event. He was wonderfully tall, with a charmingly large schnozz and a smile to match, and he laughed at my jokes. We exchanged cards, businesslike. When it came time to leave, the friend I was with encouraged me to go and say goodbye, maybe suggest that we get together. "He was clearly into you!" she prodded.

I stared at him across the party, and really wanted to. I watched the way he threw his head back when he laughed, how warm and open he was with everyone he talked to, and I felt swoony. But there was no way. I could not summon the beast, could not prod her out of her cage. So I left, feeling vaguely defeated by my lack of gumption.

What had happened to me? Xandra's words got my head in a spin. There was no big breakup that sent my lioness back into the jungle, no deaths, no major insults to my psyche. I suspect there are a million small reasons—as simple as having gained a few extra pounds, and as complicated as cultural obsession with youth. I ticked off a few in my head, and they began to add up.

- Nowadays, at social gatherings, men look past me to younger women (the large-nosed Laughing Man notwithstanding). It happens to everyone my age. It's endemic.

- Women my age in Hollywood films play mothers and aunts and even independent spinsters, but rarely sexual beings (one exception being Diane Keaton in *Something's Gotta Give*, God bless her).

- My most recent flame, a guy in his mid-fifties, told me he has a new, twenty-five-year-old girlfriend. That's right, my daughter's age. Ouch. Pass the Geritol and the Botox.

- Two of my former May-December beaus (both at least fifteen years younger than me) are also now going out with women young enough to be my daughter. One of them, for Christ's sake, actually expressed interest in her.

- Makeup ads that boast of eradicating wrinkles use models who have thirty years to go before they get one.

- Hormones wreak havoc with both the mind and the body. I just don't crave sex like I used to.

- Nothing kills fearlessness like the acquisition of a little wisdom. For example, I never had a problem going to bed with an ex, under mutually agreeable circumstances. But in recent years, I have thought, what's the point? He'll be back to his life tomorrow, and how will mine be enriched?

But I have to say, losing my roar does not mean that all the changes have been negative. I consider it a sign of my self-sufficiency, and also of a damn good life, overall, that I have not been grieving the fade. At fifty, I am happier than ever before, reveling in rich creative and intellectual pursuits. And in the company of my friends.

In fact, I've been spending so much time with my women friends in recent years that I have not even always noticed the dateless phases. Being single, after two bad marriages and innumerable disappointing affairs, mostly feels like a luxury. But *everyone* —even if she doesn't feel the urge to marry again—needs occasional contact with bare skin; everyone wants to be told she is adored and sexy. And that's something I have not had in too long.

"I have to admit it," I told Xandra. "Not being sought after anymore has done a number on my self-esteem. It's hard to even remember what it was like to feel desirable."

"Well, wait a minute," she challenged. "Why do you give your self-esteem away to men? Why do you let them take it? You're great at your job, you have great friends—doesn't that count for anything?"

"Yes, it counts for a lot," I conceded. "I feel good about all those things as a female human being. But as a sexual being? Jesus, I feel completely out of touch with my inner harlot. It's almost impossible to imagine getting laid anymore."

"Well, my friend." Xandra sat back in her chair. "Clearly you have psyched yourself out. Women don't have to buy into the Hollywood version of what 'sexy' is, you know that. You need to turn that attitude around!"

"But how?" I sighed. "It's so daunting, Xandra. Maybe I should just chalk it up to shifting priorities and call it a sex life."

I mean, I had always thought that I would, at some point, relax into better manners. Become less interested in male conquest and more interested in bird-watching and foreign films, maybe take up some kind of hobby that required yarn. But somehow I always thought all that could transpire around age seventy, not fifty.

Maybe karma is at work here, I thought. Maybe the cavalier way I used to treat men has caught up to me with a vengeance. In the past, I always knew if one guy didn't work out, there would be another the following week. I was terrible at seeing a relationship through, always bailed when things got difficult. Perhaps, cosmically, it's only fair that I pay for my sins with an early retirement from love and sex . . .

Ah, who was I kidding? The truth was, the lioness retreated because I let her go. I bought the bullshit—all the outside-imposed reasons for not staying in the game. In reality, women my age still make conquests, flirt, and have meaningful, if not lifetime-lasting, sex. And they don't even have to be a size four to do it. Look at Liz Taylor, Joan Collins, Kathy Bates. Look at Susan Sarandon, frequently photographed lip-locking her hunky, decade-younger husband. Look at Jane Juska, who, as her recent memoir recounts, was sixty-six when she placed an erotic (and amazingly effective) personals ad in the *New York Review of Books*.

Maybe it was time to reassess. To take a crash course in self-esteem repair. To vault back onto the horse (so to speak).

"Thank you for bringing this up," I told Xandra as the check arrived. "Obviously I need to take some drastic action here."

"Like what?" she inquired, smiling. "You already have all the raw material in place."

"That's right, I do!" I said quickly, my spirits rising by the second. "I don't know exactly *what* I'll do, but I've got to climb out of this! Go back to the health club, because I feel better all around when I work out. Eat more vegetables. Get some hot new boots for fall. Stop letting the world dictate my self-esteem."

I paused. "Bring the lioness out of retirement."

When I got home, I pulled out Laughing Man's business card and sent him an e-mail. An hour later, I had a date for Saturday night.

I could feel the roar start to rise in my throat.

Adventures in Cyber Snatching

Marcelle Karp

"**P**ix": *Doused in patchouli, he had driven his beat-up Volkswagen all the way from Baltimore to my place in New York City for what would prove to be our one and only get-together. Perhaps, to cover up the musk-and-gasoline odor of his car, he'd overcompensated when he was freshening up. Whatever. The scent of a woman or a man is a massive dating deal breaker for me, but patchouli is the worst offender. Its aroma took over this encounter, and I was repelled. Still, I didn't want to waste my date time, so I suggested a shower. Pix's face went Cheshire Cat on me until I explained that I didn't need the shower; he did, if we were going to get jiggy with it.*

Descented, he was in almost good enough shape for a nose dive to my pleasure zone. I weighed the options: to have sex or not to have sex. Well, Pix was there, and I was horny. I burned seven sticks of sandalwood incense, simultaneously, for our union.

I was once a woman on a mission: to spread the word of the pleasure principle, the relentless and single-minded goal of sexual satisfaction—with or without a partner—to every female being in the world. As one of the two founders of *BUST*, a feminist 'zine that grew in cup sizes over the years, I discovered that women desperately needed to know how to get off.

Certainly females were familiar with coitus; it was the finer points of self-stimulation that some of our sisters seemed to gloss over. At *BUST*, we constantly urged women to introduce themselves to a vibrator, to find that sexual healing power in their dominant hand, to stop relying on a partner to get them to the holy O. I practiced what I preached. My vibrator was my best friend, but I also bedded babe-alicious boys and girls all over the world, sometimes without taking a number and other times falling so hard I had a hard time seeing straight.

The dalliance with the Surfer Fox I met on holiday in Australia turned into a whirlwind lust fest. A year later, after moving to New York to be with me, he was back on a plane to the Land Down Under. I was relieved to be rid of him, but I was soon late on my period. The pee test was pink and positive, and while he screamed *Abort! Abort! Abort!* via international phone calls and e-mail, I felt differently.

Oh, I wanted this child from the moment I knew she existed in my body; I morphed instantly into that cliché, the Glowing Pregnant Lady, tossing around eyeball-rolling epithets ("This is the most beautiful experience, ever!") without one hint of irony. My libidinous surges were nonexistent, almost unheard of for a pregnant woman (not to mention for *me*). And I didn't even care, because I felt like such a gorgeous, invincible goddess. I, the ravenous predator of willies, the woman with an apartment that resembled a stop-and-go, had gone goo-goo ga-ga.

It was, in some ways, easier being a knocked-up single chick without the Inseminator around. But he turned up on my doorstep the week before the baby was born. We married a month later, for resident status purposes more than from a deep longing to be together forever. He wanted to be a part of the baby's life, I wanted the helping hand, and the visa people wanted to deport aliens, unless they were hitched to true blue Americans.

Once I met my daughter, Ruby, I lost interest in the other baby I'd created, *BUST*. I only wanted to watch Ruby's neck loll about or analyze the texture of her pesto-colored poo. I was annoyed when the office rang, wanting to know when I was coming back. Coming back? Hell, to what? Arguing whether or not a vibrator in the shape of a gun was feminist? I had it all, right in front of me. For me, becoming a mother was the be-all and end-all. Becoming a wife was another story. It—married-ness with Him—sucked.

Our marital bliss was more like a marital hiss; we were combustible, except within the confines of the boudoir, where we were addictively and confusingly explosive. My libido demanded make-up time for its nine-month hiatus and my husband was a panting participant, hungry as I was for nonspeaking intimacy. As I puttered around the house in a silk teddy, he would change diapers with one hand, play "hey diddle diddle" on me with the other. Our sexual life was wild and woozy and without limits, but our love life was turbulent and toxic and suffocating.

And, by Ruby's second birthday, it was over.

Suddenly single again, but now with a demanding toddler in full-time tow, I was in dire need of some tender loving care. Or, at the very least, some unbridled lust. I knew, both instinctively and from experience, that there was only one sure restorative for my damaged sense of self: sex, and plenty of it. Not necessarily earth-shattering sex; more like outlet sex. Without expectation, without guilt. I needed to look into a new lover's eyes and see hunger—for me. I needed to be surprised by a man's package, to be aroused by a woman's touch. I needed to objectify, to use, to feed, over and over, without apology. I needed to address my most base instincts, not forever, but for as long as it took to recover my sense of self—and I didn't want to be on trial for it.

In pre-baby days, whenever I felt that certain Southern itch, finding a temporary salve was easy. I just "went out," always returning with the needed antidote. But that was then. Now, as a thirty-eight-year-old Mama Bear, I was encumbered. With child, without child support. With debts, without employment. With baggage, without a net. Perhaps most problematic of all, as a married woman, I'd forsaken the coquette in me, putting all my energy and love into nurturing my child and partner. I'd become a master at the art of pleasing, not teasing. I'd lost my predatory edge. My dormant bad-ass self needed resurrection, and fast.

Still, what was I going to do? Run out and pick a random "victim" for fornication purposes only? I needed a game plan.

The funny thing about submerging your head in baby goo is that you lose touch with the world you once knew. I'd heard stories through the non-mommy grapevine about online dating, the hot new way to hook up. But I had no idea of the extent of the explosion, how thoroughly the game had gone cyber. And if you believed the latest statistic from *U.S. News & World Report*, I was not the only person in dating land scratching her head. As of October 2003, forty million Americans had checked out one of the myriad matchmaking sites that had suddenly mushroomed on the Web. Online dating had become the New Black, the New Britney, the New Beginning.

And soon I, too, was a new beginner. While Ruby napped one afternoon, I made good use of the downtime to check out the online singles scene for myself. From the privacy and safety of my bedroom, I perused JPEG after JPEG of online personals, flitting from site to site as the impulse struck. And what a cornucopia of sites there were—a niche to suit every taste. For more or less conventional dating, there was Match.com. For the girl in search of that nice Jewish doctor, there was JDate.com. Those who thought of themselves as hipsters would probably prowl Nerve. Even generic pop culture Web sites, like Media Bistro and Gawker, provided links to online dating. Ivy League alumni, I discovered, could continue on the exclusive road to elitism with Ivydaters.com. Bespectacled babes might find themselves bethrothed at guysmakepassesatgirlswhowearglasses.com. I halfway expected to find a site devoted to those who would only date horse owners.

It didn't take long, though, to figure out that the men and women I might soon be meeting were looking for just one thing, no matter which of the three standard descriptions they used in their ads—"dating" (i.e., sex), "play" (i.e., sex), "serious relationship" (yeah, right). But the fact that online "dating" was a euphemism for ACTION, the same way as walking into a bar is a sign that you're out on the sniff, suited me just fine. I wasn't ready for love; I was, really and only, up for a love tap.

"Chica": She was babbling in her thick Italian accent about Wonder Woman as the quintessential feminist icon, but I couldn't hear her; I could only feel desire pulsating in the place where I wake warm. On a self-absorbed roll, she didn't notice as I leaned in and inhaled her. Ten years my junior, and half a foot taller— hot. She had never heard of Bread or Styx or the Misfits—standard dating deal breakers. Still, she wore Shalimar. All I wanted was to bury my face where she pressed her thighs tight.

Sex that night was no different than with any of my male cyber dates; it was quick and urgent, and I could walk away without turning into a repeat customer. Chica was the first person I met online whose appetite came close to mine; too bad she had no taste in music.

The problem for many a solo parent is how to get some when your child lives in the next room. My ex and I agreed that Ruby could have an overnight in his rundown tenement apartment one night a week. In theory, this meant that I had one opportunity a week to get laid. But motherhood, the need to protect my young daughter from any fallout from my sex life, imposed even further restrictions. *No sleepovers while Ruby is in the house. No action whatsoever while Ruby is in the house. No introducing my playmates to Ruby until certain words of love and commitment are exchanged.* (Of course, this last was more a theoretical than a practical concern, considering that my game plan was simply to use and discard.)

Plus, even *I* didn't want to blow every second of my minimal non-mommy time on blow jobs. Shooting the shit with my girl-friends has always been one of my favorite pastimes; thus, I reserved all but one of my child-free nights each month for Girls Night Out. Sometimes, though, hanging out with my female friends was more taxing than a date with a Jersey guy soaked in Paco Rabanne.

"What, you're just fucking for the sake of it?" they'd ask me.

"Yeah."

"Don't you want to make love with someone you like?"

"Sure I do. But I don't have to like everyone I have sex with. And I definitely wouldn't call it 'making love.'" And this is where I would completely lose them. "It's just, you know, sex."

"Just sex? What about love and commitment? Doesn't it feel empty?"

"No," I'd retort, "it feels fucking good."

Really, this Victorian line of questioning puzzled me. In the old days, my friends, even the swingers who were always out all night, lived vicariously through my tales of erotic exploits. But now they raised plucked eyebrows, occasionally "tsk"-ing at my new method of meeting sex partners. Had they forgotten that I'd always been all about promoting pleasure for women, or did they think that my convictions would fade as I aged? Did they really find it more acceptable to stalk sexual prey at a party than online? Was it because I was now a mother that they questioned why I would have sex with anyone who wasn't relationship material?

Of course, no one in my circle of cohorts had been with my ex, and few of them had child-imposed restrictions on their dating lives as I did. Given the emotional and physical parameters of my post-divorce life, I thought I was doing pretty well. No matter what else anyone might say, I was playing and living by my own standards!

"Sven": Two drinks in, I finally noticed it, something glistening in the dim light of the bar on his left hand, fourth finger. The ring finger. But his profile hadn't mentioned a wife. Okay, okay, Married People masquerading as The Unattached happens, but still. Still! The guy had claimed that he was seeking a "serious relationship" in his online profile. Damn it, he was cute too, with long, thick fingers and a shoe size of eleven . . . usually sure signs that a guy is packing. My one night a month to have fun and there I was, saddled atop my moral high horse. Oh, well. I was hungry, but I wasn't starving. When Sven excused himself for a bathroom break, I made a break as well—out of there.

The beauty of online dating was that I didn't have to invest my precious time and energy in seduction. I could cut to the chase, simply get off with an animate object du jour, the way men have been doing since time immemorial. I took phone numbers but never gave my home phone or even my last name. I flaked on meetings if the spirit didn't move me, rejected unsuitable prospects (like Sven) on the spot, shot off mean e-mails saying that I saw no need for a second date. Despite, or because of, this bad behavior, I was desired. Bouquets, lingerie, and invitations for repeat dates all flowed my way. For a time, the cyber world provided exactly what I needed.

I'd be lying, though, if I claimed that there is no downside to the responsible pursuit of the casual fuck. The truth is, I swore off cyber dating after an encounter that disgusted me so deeply on an aesthetic level that I didn't have sex again for two entire months. When I finally did, it was with someone I cared about, a Southern gentleman I'd met through work, who courted me so sweetly I couldn't resist. Wrapped in his arms, I knew I was finally healed, ready to move on to pleasures of a different kind.

Certainly, if a man were to reveal a similar story to me, I'd call him a pig, castigate him for treating women disrespectfully, chastise him for acting like . . . a man. But now I understand why guys do this, why sex is only sex for them. Because sometimes that's all it is. Only sex. Of course it's thrilling when the passion between two people is more than just physical. But when true love isn't knocking at your door, true sluttishness might just be what the doctor ordered. In approaching sex like a man—clearly and simply for pleasure—I protected and bolstered my ego, sidestepping the emotional pitfalls that my postdivorce pscyhe just wasn't ready to handle. And, as I found my sex-for-sex's-sake online rhythm, I regained faith in myself. Faith in the spunky sexpot I had always been, but faith also in the baby-besotted mother who had gambled for "happily ever after" and lost. Faith in myself as a woman who was ultimately on a quest for love, but didn't mind (not in the least) getting salaciously sidetracked for a year.

It's A Doggie Dog World

Cynthia Heimel

*A*re dogs ever mentally ill? Well, sure. Look at my beautiful rottweiler-beagle. Stare into her big brown poignant eyes. Try to pat her on the head. Go ahead, try.

Dorothy was found wandering in the road, almost getting hit by cars. She was taken to the Milo Foundation, an excellent animal refuge in Mendocino County, California. That's where I found her. She was a fat girl, running in circles. I identified completely. When I took her for a walk, she kept her head down and her ears flattened. At every odd noise or slightly erratic movement, she flinched. She was a walking tic; so, of course, I took her home to be my foster dog. When she got more socialized, I would find her a permanent home. Or so I thought.

When we got home, Dorothy immediately ran out the back door and under the house, where she lived for a month. I would set out bowls of food; she would wait until I was back inside, rush out, inhale the food, and run back to her lair.

Yes, Dorothy was completely mentally ill. She was unstable, nonfunctioning, paranoid, and totally, utterly freaked. Somebody in her past had really liked hitting her. She is still somewhat scared of hands—especially if those hands pick something up. Then she goes running, running, running.

A little while after I got Dorothy, I hit my head in an elevator accident, which caused a post-concussive syndrome and a total breakdown. I lay on the couch all day, wrapped up in blankets even though it was hot outside. I was unstable, nonfunctioning, paranoid, and totally, utterly freaked. People had to stay with me in case I tried to kill myself.

Dorothy came out from under the house and gradually started making appearances inside, slithering in through the back door. If anyone was with me, she'd disappear. But if I was alone, Dorothy would approach me. One day she put her head under my hand for a pat. Then, a few weeks later, she started kissing my hand. In a few weeks more, she started kissing my face.

We soaked up each other's affection like two mentally ill sponges. After three months, Dorothy sat by my side for hours at a time, giving me the dog saliva cure. I whispered to her over and over, "What a good girl, what a pretty girl, what a silly baby." She loved the nonsense syllables. She would look deep into my eyes, then leap into the air and kiss me.

Finally, she let other people put a leash on her and take her for a walk. This was a big step. I was inspired to go along for the walks. This was also a big step.

One day, I got up, put a flowered yellow ribbon in my hair for no reason, and took Dorothy for a stroll around the block—just the two of us. Although I felt completely unsafe, I was hell-bent on doing it. We started out slowly, taking little steps. While we walked, I suddenly realized she was carefully placing herself between me and other pedestrians.

This terrified nutcase was putting herself closer to terrifying humans—for me! I walked a little more confidently. I straightened the goofy, hopeful ribbon in my hair. We were almost giddy by the time we returned home.

Two years later, neither of us is nearly as mentally ill as we once were, and she's nobody's foster dog. She's my dog.

2.

Attitude Adjustment

Reality is something you rise above.

—Liza Minnelli

My Buddies the Oysters

Ms. Gonick

It's one thing to go to college when you're eighteen and still have the innocence of one of Lewis Carroll's famed baby oysters; it's another to return when you're fifty-one and have long since turned into his Walrus. If I'd only had the sense to turn into his Carpenter instead, I wouldn't have had to go back at all. I'd be working a union job blessed with full benefits, owning a residence instead of just renting, and be free of the consequences of landlordian whims.

As it was, the owner of the perfect rent-controlled apartment in which I'd lived for twenty-one years had decided to sell the building to someone (no doubt a carpenter) who'd be tearing it down to put up a new one to sell for a very fat profit. In a race against time and a wrecking ball, I knew I couldn't afford to move anywhere that wasn't a gutter unless I secured a grown-up career. (Freelance writing is only grown-up if you're married to someone who can pick up the slack.) I decided I'd make a great high school English teacher, being both literate and bossy, and rushed to my alma mater to enroll in its credential program.

In my panic for solvency, I forgot two things: (1) I hadn't been in a college classroom for twenty-nine years, or high school for a mere thirty-three, and, like the world, both had changed; (2) I was not just any walrus, but a walrus with a brain tumor (a right-sided acoustic neuroma) that had spent the last decade eating half my hearing and balance. Radiated to death two years earlier, it was no longer a threat to my brain stem, and knowing this was such a relief that I didn't even think about radiation's aftereffects.

And why should I? I was armed with a new life-saving plan, which I proudly put into effect in the fall semester of 2001. My old campus no longer had hippies, but it did have sushi, which was a nice change, and I'd made some young friends (who really *were* oysters), which was also a change.

Then, of course, the real change came when the towers came down.

It's beyond bratty to say that the events of September 11 dampened my enthusiasm for school, so I'll say this instead: I didn't know I'd *had* any enthusiasm till after it left and it seemed to do so just post 9/11. Then again, its disappearance might have been due to the shift into fall, the getting dark at six, the lonely lurch to the parking lot after a night class, the standard check for the backseat rapist (now rapist/terrorist) before unlocking the car, the hallucinatory drive home (night vision iffy), the anthrax reports on the radio.

Whatever the reason, distinguishing verbal phrases from adjective clauses suddenly felt existentially stupid, like Lucy and Ethel in the chocolate factory trying to prove they could work in a chocolate factory. With WWIII coming, I no longer thought about teaching Camus (high school students still read *L'Etranger*); I felt something had turned me *into* Camus and that I, too, was stuffing bonbons beneath my beret as hundreds more sailed right past me. It got to the point where I thought I should just drop out, lie down, and *eat* the damn chocolates—with litres of absinthe of course, and a tin plate to hold the butts *de Gauloise* I'd chainsmoke to the tunes of Edith Piaf while waiting for the end to come. In Paris, preferably, but since that would mean flying, I supposed right here would do.

But because it was too late in the term (not to mention my life) to drop out of anything, I had my new study group come over instead. We were going to bone up on grammar, but since the four of them were still babes in their twenties, and oysters at that, we mostly ate Cheetos and talked about sex. Or rather, they talked about sex while I, who'd spent forty years eschewing the Cheeto—not to mention the Screaming Yellow Zonker my stoned generation (who'd actually *invented* sex so this one could talk about it) had devoured in college—ate half a bagful and opened another.

The conversation was very confusing.

"Friends with deficits?" I asked, echoing Miriam, who'd just been explaining how she managed sex when she didn't have a boyfriend or girlfriend. "What does that mean?"

Sam, my audio interpreter, wrote *Benefits* on my exercise book.

"Oh," I said. "Benefits." Pause. "Huh?"

"Sex," Sam said into my left ear. "Secks," he repeated to make sure I got it. I heard him but I still didn't get it.

"Buddies," declared Miriam, *"you can also have sex with."*

"With whom you can also have sex," I corrected, since this was a grammar group, and then I heard what I'd said and was horrified.

"Why would you have sex with a buddy?" I asked.

"No complications," an oyster explained.

"No ties," said another. "No expectations. No disappoint-ments."

As these last two were boysters, I wasn't surprised, but I couldn't believe it of Miriam. Sex without drama? What was the point?

"So it's kind of like, what, working out?" I asked. "With your buddy?"

All four of them nodded.

"So you're hanging out with your buddy and then you get bored but you can't find a good movie and the pizza's not there yet so you just sort of decide to pass time having sex?"

They nodded.

"Miriam?" I said, giving her a dubious look.

"Really!" she said, nodding and grinning.

I went to the kitchen to pour my diet Coke down the drain and came back with a full glass of wine.

"It's absinthe," I told them. "I'm too old to live."

A few days later I was walking to class weighing the pros and cons of hanging out with the young (*pro:* they're not homeowners either; *con:* depressing buddy revelations) when I *truly* became too old to live, or in any case, too insane to walk.

As my neurosurgeon would explain to me later, another festive side effect of brain radiation (besides the festive facial tics I was already enjoying) is an ataxic gait that, just like the tics, is almost always brought on by stress. Since ataxia (from the Greek *ataktos*: *a* for *not* and *taktos* for *ordered*) means "loss or lack of muscular coordination" and gait means gait, an ataxic gait means your walk gets disordered. The first time it happened, it got so disordered it went out of order entirely, like an elevator that stops between floors and refuses to budge till the Otis man comes. I was in between steps when my right foot, suddenly and without so much as a quiver of warning, decided to glue itself to the ground.

I kept trying to lift it and it kept resisting. When I finally realized I wasn't *able* to lift it, an instinctive vanity made me pretend that *of course I was able* (*un*able being too close to *dis*abled for *this* narcissist), but had chosen instead to stand in one place because it was better for thinking deep thoughts.

And I did think a deep thought: *Has biochemical warfare struck the west coast or am I standing in gum?*

I looked around to see if anyone else on campus looked paralyzed, but they were all using both feet to zip this way and that and I didn't see any gas masks. Nor, unfortunately, did I see any of the oysters from my pretend-to-study-grammar group. Demented as they might be (about romance, that is, and I blamed my own generation for that as we were the first to say, "Wanna ball?"), they were the only friends I'd made since returning to school, and if just one of them noticed me waving and yelling, I felt sure I could get him to yank my right foot out of its glue and carry me piggyback to my next class. (Another *pro* for hanging out with the young: Strong; might help with paralysis.)

Alas, there was nary an oyster, not even a clam. I waved and yelled to everyone else, but as they were all using their cell phones (except for those using headphones), they were staring into that middle distance where no real human contact is made. School banners still shouted *Connect* and *Reflect* and, most unctuous of all, *Love Is Stronger Than Hate,* but let me tell you right now: forget the Siren, the Harpy, the Wild—nothing is stronger than the call of the cell. If Horton the elephant had gotten a cell phone (and surely he has at least seven by now), I was the last *Who* left in *Who*-ville screaming in vain for his attention.

Luckily, just thinking of being the last *Who* in *Who*-ville (a sort of nuclear, lonely, *On the Beach* thought) made my right eye so nervous it started to twitch, and this reminded me that telling myself I had lots of money had once calmed it down and made the twitch stop. Deciding this foot thing probably stemmed from a neuro situation as well (right-sided tumor, right eye, right foot), I made myself think of a new soothing myth, and here it is in case your foot ever glues itself to the ground:

I wasn't alone on a lawn on a campus, but standing beside my own neurosurgeon who had abandoned his entire life as he'd known it to devote himself to my post-op wellbeing. Insisting on never leaving my side (my left one, so I could hear his continuing words of praise and encouragement), he not only diagnosed my side effects as they occurred, he made them irrelevant by swooping me up in his huge hairy arms and carrying me to my next destination.

And, by the way, I still had lots of money and we were sailing to Paris to eat duck confit and wait *a deux* for the end.

I called this one: *Fay Neuro Wray and Dr. King Kong.*

Or: *The Kongs Go to France and OD on Absinthe.*

If you're insane enough, tricks like this work. Like Prometheus unglued, I brushed myself off and lurched onward to class.

Foreign Correspondent

Cynthia Kaplan

Perhaps it is a result of the astonishing surfeit of survival shows on TV, or the fifteen-year-old holiday card I came across recently depicting my husband and his buddy, Bill, in hiking boots and do-rags, astride motorcycles in some remote corner of Thailand, or perhaps it is my secret love for expensive performance outerwear, but it has suddenly occurred to me that I may never have an adventure in a foreign country. I didn't have the guts to do it in college or in my twenties and now that I feel ready it's too late because I'm saddled with the husband and children I always wanted. And, coincidentally, as if the point needed hammering home, I seem just as suddenly to be finding myself in conversations with people who once lived in a hut at the base of Kilimanjaro, or hiked across Indonesia with only a Nikormat and a spoon, or thumbed their way through Ireland, getting thrown out of pubs and occasionally subbing for a local football club—people who dedicated a reasonable period of their young adulthood to adventure travel, the upshot being that their minds are expanded, their bodies possessed of certain intangible but unimpeachable foreign sense memories, their photo albums of serious interest. They are semifluent in several languages and have acquired a bevy of international friends and acquaintances whom they will visit and who will visit them for the rest of their natural lives. When you talk to them, all their sentences begin with "I met

Dominique in Budapest . . . " and end with " . . . so we climbed Machu Picchu."

Some of their adventures were actually altruistic. These trips were about following their conscience, wherever it took them. I didn't have any of those either. In the past three months alone I have discovered that friends of mine variously taught elementary school in the Congo, built bridges in Nicaragua, and gave out eyeglasses to impoverished Mayans. *Their* sentences begin with, "Then, when we were with Medicins Sans Frontiers, sorry, that's Doctors Without Borders, . . . " and end with, " . . . so that year we spent Christmas handing out Hershey bars to orphans in Colombia . . . sorry, it's just . . . (sob)."

Until now, it has never occurred to me to climb Machu Picchu, much less join the Peace Corps. Extreme altitudes make my head ache, and I have an irrational fear of reactionaries armed with machetes. While I have rallied to a number of causes I believed in, none of those rallies took me beyond a three-mile radius of my home, unless you count the address on the envelope the check is in. I've never even worked on a political campaign, stumping around my *own* country, staying up all night to make signs or cold calls or blow up balloons. I didn't meet my husband at a caucus. I've signed a few petitions in my time, but I never traveled by bus to Washington and stood in the rain on the Mall waiting for Jessie Jackson to speechify or Pete Seeger to sing. I did stand all night in a freezing rain outside Madison Square Garden waiting for Springsteen tickets to go on sale. He sings that old song about war.

Anecdotally speaking—and what other way of speaking is there, really—I have nothing to offer these buccaneers in return. Which I resent. What else do humans do besides sit around and tell stories that make them look cool? (I've never heard of a *dog* rhapsodizing about a three-year tour teaching English as a second language to children in Mauritius. " . . . *And by then the flood waters were as high as the tree stumps they use for desks! Woof!*") So what I usually do instead, because I don't want to be left out of the conversation, is make a big deal about some little event, tell a grandiose tale of a weekend spent car-camping or hunting for old doorknobs or some other pointless endeavor. And I put a funny spin on it. *"Then there was the time at the party for Bob's seventy-fifth birthday when my hair was attacked by a horde of freaked-out Luna moths. Hah hah hah."* Woof.

I am sure it is horrible when the only route out of the ancient ruins is washed away in a mudslide, and one might certainly have second thoughts about one's calling after moving to a third-world country and wearing the same pair of underpants for a week while digging irrigation ditches. But there must be—or they all wouldn't talk about it so much—an enormous sense of accomplishment at having done it, survived it. I've seen the looks of pride on the mud-covered faces in the photographs, the shit-eating grins and sinewy, tanned bodies. (Sound romantic? Does to me!) The wages of sweat equity.

And the wages pay dividends. For years to come these world travelers/do-gooders will dine out on their stories, and we do-nothings, with neither the experiences nor the tales they inspire, will listen with a mixture of envy and annoyance.

I did not grow up in an adventurous family. We never went camping out West or took a sabbatical in New Zealand or walked the Appalachian Trail calling each other by our trail names: Gopher, Birdman, Princess Pine, Cranky Cuss. Neither my brother nor I was sent to live on a kibbutz and harvest olives, which I am not even adventurous enough to like. I grew up in a family where the adventures were, thank God, *tuh tuh tuh*, over by the time my parents were born. *Their* parents had made the arduous trip from the Old World to the New World and that was certainly enough adventure travel as far as everyone was concerned. They had risked their lives for us, and now we owed it to them to just stay home and enjoy the fact that we have carpeting.

When my mother finished college, her parents sent her, with two friends, on the grand tour of Europe. All their hotels and flights were arranged in advance. During the day they went to museums, and at night to restaurants where they wore white gloves on their hands and foreign boys politely asked them to dance. The single story that has endured lo these many years is the one about the evening in Paris when my mother's best friend Sugar Silverman, who preferred her hair jet black, colored the light roots with an eyebrow pencil before going out. She danced all night long with her head nestled on the shoulder of a young Frenchman and left a large dark splotch on his white dinner jacket.

My legacy.

Unfortunately, my subsequent experience of *la vie Française* lacked something, or, really, everything, of the romance so fondly recalled by my mother. In the winter of my junior year in high school, I lived with a family in France as an exchange student for a month. I was the only student whose correspondent was of the opposite sex, and we didn't exactly bond. He did not find me attractive enough to try to have sex with, and I was obsessed with the fact that he wore the same outfit to school for an entire week. Everyone else became best friends with their host and even shared clothes, which, given what I now knew about French habits of dress, seemed inexplicable. Still, the girls walked to school arm in arm, in the French style, and I trailed Jacques by several *metres*. They were having a different experience than I was, a happy one, a freeing one, and it ignited in them dually an urge to travel and a sense of (perhaps) belonging somewhere other than Connecticut. Some of them got Eurail passes and spent the summers hopping from city to city, seeing the sights, making friends, and having sex with men with foreign accents. One girl moved to France for the rest of her life. She became an *"expat."* In literature, expats always seem to lead groovy, romantic, if slightly seedy, Somerset Maugham lives. They learn the language, eat sweetbreads, shower less often. When this girl came home for the holidays, her conversation was sprinkled with clever little foreign expressions. *Mon cher. Tant pis. Merde.*

What has stayed with me, all these years later—a tiny souvenir of my brief sojourn in France—is Florence. Florence was Jacques' little sister. And while I remember little of her actual personage, and have no particular reminiscences of our relationship, sometimes her name just comes to me, out of nowhere. Not Florence as *we* say it (FLOOR-ence) but Florence in the French way: Floor-AHNCE-uh. Floor-AHNCE-uh.

Another obstacle to my global emancipation was that sometime in my late teens I developed a fear of flying. I actually pray upon take-off and landing, a hedge against the unimaginableslashimaginable. How is it that we just get on airplanes, tra-la-la, as though it doesn't require, if we think about it for a *second*, a breath-stopping, life-shortening expense of will to suspend disbelief? I could have been hit by the Eighty-Sixth Street Crosstown any day, so I guess I didn't see the point of torturing myself with a fifteen-hour plane ride to some remote destination, what with the avalanches and the leeches, when I could just as easily meet my maker here, at home, where it's safe.

And it's not just that I was afraid to travel, I was also afraid to actually *leave*. I was sure that if I left my little life, such as it was, something amazing would go on while I was gone. That the life that I had always hoped to live would suddenly start while I wasn't there. Party invitations would come in, men would call for dates, last-minute performance opportunities attended by influential people would materialize. Of course, I stayed home a lot and none of this ever transpired. When I moved to New York after college to pursue an acting career, *that*, ostensibly, in the eyes of my family, which is what the word ostensibly secretly means, was adventure aplenty. Add four years of waiting tables (an occupation that one's status as an Ivy League graduate does not prepare one's parents for), and I might as well have just ripped up the carpeting and caught the next boat back to Odessa, having ground the wheels of progress to a virtual halt. Although, ironically, a trip to Odessa would not be entirely out of context with my current thinking.

In college, when other people were making plans to take a semester abroad, I assumed that if I left for that long I'd lose all my friends, or they'd become better friends with each other than they were with me, which I think they were anyway. They'd have all these outrageous experiences, urban-myth-forming experiences, experiences they'd spend the rest of college reminding each other of and laughing about in front of me. I wasn't just paranoid. All I had to do was go to *sleep*, and life happened without me. One cold winter night, after I'd yawned myself back to my room off campus, four of my friends ventured out in the predawn freeze to paint the front steps of a house on Spruce Street pink and green, a mock tribute to the preppy boys who lived there. This prank became something of a legend that was told and retold for years after. Often people assumed I'd been involved, and I did not dispossess them of this notion.

Strangely, none of the men I know who are husbands and fathers feel the same way—that they missed out on something important, perhaps mind-altering or life-changing, before they settled down. They don't want to be anyplace or anyone other than where and who they are (except, maybe, on a tropical island, divorced, with hair) because they did the big things first. And perhaps they were able to do those things because, and here we go, there was no pressure on them to find mates and to get their careers started so they could have babies before the freshness date on their eggs expired. No one worries about men going the distance alone until they are, say, forty-five, and even then, they shake their heads and smile, *the ol' gad-about*. Besides, sperm have the same half-life as a sea turtle, somewhere between eighty years and oblivion. Of course, women, too, go on trips and to graduate school and have careers, but in the back of their minds (and if I'm not talking about you, or if you've read any of the three gazillion books recently written on this subject, feel free to skip this part) they are tormented by the presence of a very persistent voice, a *nudge*. The nudge, who might sound a bit like your mother—that's not uncommon—says that it's fine to venture out into the world and make something of yourself but while you're at it you should get married and stay home and have kids. The nudge understands the desire for freedom but is having a hard time living the dream. And the worst part is that the nudge speaks a modicum of truth: you can't argue with biology.

Now that I actually have, among other things, two ravishing children, meaning, I don't need to hang around trying to *get* them anymore, something else quite remarkable has happened. My fear of mudslides, guerillas, et al., has disappeared. My body as I've known it has evaporated into the cosmos, and its particles have been reconfigured and it has returned, postpartum, as the force field from *Lost in Space*. My fear for my own safety has been supplanted by my fear for that of my children. The old worries have been replaced by an entirely new set, wherein windpipe-sized gumballs, nippy schnauzers, and desperate, childless strangers lurking in department stores top the list. My job now is to protect my children, not myself, except to the extent that I, the force field, am obliged to remain alive and well and in the general vicinity of said children in order to be effective. But, also, or rather, more to the point, I have begun to imagine myself to be, in my new, unselfconscious manifestation, a buccaneer. Handing out eyeglasses. Joining that club for polar explorers. Flying on airplanes. As long as my children are safely on the ground, well, tra la la.

This revelation may account for the feeling I now have that I've been living in a snow globe. Maybe the kind with music, sure, but I have been, for most of my life, happy to look out on the world from the relative safety of my winter wonderland and gasp with amazement and admiration at the derring-do of others, at their selflessness, at the ease with which they have inhabited the *real* globe. While I wouldn't trade my life right now for (almost) anyone else's, I'll say this, though it was recently the plot of a failed sitcom: I wish I could take how far I've come and go back to where I was, just for a little while. Or what if there was a Narnia for grown-ups? I recently reread the *Chronicles*, to see if they were really as boring as I remembered them, and they were, but there is something to the idea that you could disappear into a wardrobe or a painting or a door in the sky and spend months, if not years, on an adventure and then come back having missed only about ten seconds of your real life.

Or perhaps I would simply be gratified by some kind of retroactive inclusion in the occasional anecdote, if once in a while at a social gathering a friend said something like, "Hey, Cin, remember when we were holed up in that lean-to on Rainier?"

Coda:

My twentieth high school reunion began auspiciously; I was having a good hair night, and in the eyes of my former classmates, it seems I had made a reasonable success of my post-adolescent life. I lived in New York City! I was a writer! And an actress! For the first time the popular boys showed some interest. (You'd think, twenty years later I'd have stopped caring, but no.) In fact, it appeared that *I* had been the adventurous one. I felt fine, virtually vindicated. A group of us settled with our drinks and hors d'oeuvres at a large round table, and everyone but me began reminiscing. I'd heard some of these stories before, and that familiarity, along with my newfound popularity, afforded me a certain license to pretend I'd been more integral to them than I actually had been. Which was not at all. I nodded and laughed along like a pro. I took big slugs of my drink and mock choked on it. Ha ha ha ha ha. It was dangerous, I knew, but I was feeling bold, even cocky, and I thought I could handle it. Which is something drunks and drug addicts say after they wake up at three in the morning in a strange city. Anyway, I should have made a break for the steam table while I had the chance.

"Remember when Peg got her head stuck in the railing at McDonald's?"

The place exploded. People could barely speak. Bits of hors d'oeuvres spewed forth. This event was obviously one of the highlights of my senior year of high school. The story, such as could be relayed between fits of coughing and howling, went like this: one autumn night, after a soccer game against New Milford, a cheerleader named Peg Sealy poked her head through the wooden railing that separated two booths at McDonald's and got it stuck there.

One of the perks of going to an away game was the opportunity to have dinner at McDonald's before the bus ride back to school. If you played field hockey or girls' basketball, as I did, there was a certain amount of female camaraderie and bonding at these dinners. They occasionally turned raucous, but, let's face it, all-girl events where neither drugs nor alcohol were present were not the stuff of legend. (As was, of course, Kathy Roger's all-girl birthday party where a cardboard tampon applicator was used as a bong. Memorable!) If you were a cheerleader, however, every away game was an actual social event. You traveled on the bus with the boys' team and then went out to dinner with them after the game. Furthermore, every game was a party to which you were required to wear a tight sweater, a very short skirt, and bobby socks. Amazingly, perhaps inevitably, it came to pass that on game days the cheerleaders wore their cheerleading outfits to school in the morning. Never in my life did I attend a party dressed like that, even on Halloween, when every girl I know dressed like a whore—not literally, but when my friends dressed as pirates, they wore eye patches, hot pants, and fishnets. They were like pirate whores. Or punk whores or flapper whores or Native American whores, whatever. The year of the pirates, junior year of college, I dressed as a St. Bernard rescue dog. God knows why. Because I was a fucking idiot, that's why. Anyway, cheerleaders are just Department of Education–endorsed Halloween whores.

But I digress. The rest of the evening I spent in a blur. The giddiness of the Peg Witnesses could not be simulated. I was a good actress, but not that good. Oddly, the seemingly central question of why Peg Sealy poked her head through the railing never came up. I realized this was because it was irrelevant. Maybe she was trying to talk to some boys at the other table, or just make a joke, but all these years later, it doesn't matter. What matters is that I, at this or any other point, would never be in the Time and Place Where Things Happen. I will most probably be stuck forever in the Place Where You Wait and Just Sort of Hope for the Best. Tigers don't change their stripes. Bearing witness to Peg Sealy's imprisonment at the New Milford McDonald's is not the herald of an adventurous life, exactly, but a connection can, and should, be made. You are either in the best yearbook group shots or not. You've either traveled to Bangladesh for the International Red Cross or not. You are the subject of the story or the unfortunate person who has to hear it over dinner. It began long, long ago and it will probably never end; it has parked itself in the cerebral cortex and erupts, like an aneurysm, at regular intervals. Right now being one of them. Key words set it off: any talk of foreign travel or selfless volunteerism, any anecdote that inspires either knee-slapping or, worse, tears. Sometimes the internal hemorrhaging starts spontaneously when I am just sitting around minding my own business, walking on the street, feeding my children, or shopping for a roll of duct tape. It floods the brain like a mantra: "Remember when Peg got her head stuck in the railing at McDonald's? Remember when Peg got her head stuck in the railing at McDonald's? REMEMBER WHEN PEG GOT HER HEAD STUCK IN THE RAILING AT MCDONALD'S?"

So what to do? While most of my peers lay awake at night conjuring images of larger apartments and luxurious vacations, I fantasize about all of the gritty, dangerous places I've never been and the perilous, character-building things I haven't done. I dream about a triumphant return to high school, although clearly it is *way* too late to learn to back-flip off a human pyramid. And maybe one day, when the kids go to college and I get a divorce, I'll embark on a journey someplace to which Jet Blue does not fly. I will get a job as a foreign correspondent, wear hiking boots and a tan vest with many pockets. There will be others of my kind, smart-talking women, and possibly men with English accents, and we will sit up at night in foreign hotel bars drinking whiskey and trading outrageous anecdotes. Oh, the stories I'll tell.

The Marvels of Middle Age

Mary Roach

Who said, "Middle age is the heinous and insidious conglomeration of small physical failings and defects that appear without warning and totally ruin your day"? It might have been me. I used to feel this way. But I have worked hard to develop a new and positive outlook about these things, which I will now share with you, so you will feel better too.

Unpigmented white spots on forearms. Compared with those little red, raised blebs on your chest and upper arms, these white spots are hardly noticeable. By the way, I'm guessing they're not only on your arms. Have you examined the fronts of your shins lately?

Red blebs on chest. These are barely visible from across a large, poorly lit room. Try to associate with people with limited vision.

Receding gums. What you are failing to realize is that the enamel underneath your gums has been protected from unsightly coffee and cigarette stains for the past thirty years and is as white and perfect as your toilet bowl above the waterline. Also, many of you have the problem of unflattering gummy smiles, and this will be alleviated by the gradual disappearance of your gums.

Crow's feet. If you've ever examined the foot of a crow up close, you'll see that the lines around your eyes, while they detract from your once-youthful looks and tend to act as foundation sinks, are not as ugly as the actual foot of a crow.

Unsightly neck cords coming down from jaw. These can easily be taken care of by cultivating a double chin. Don't want a double chin? Well today's your lucky day, because you don't have one!

Liver spots. They call them liver spots because you've lived a lot. You're a liver. If you'd done less of that living out in the sun without the good sense to put on sunscreen, you'd be a liver without spots, but never mind, too late for that now.

Yellowing toenails. Why is red a desirable toenail color and yellow not? True fact: there are yellow nail polishes one can buy, though only the young have the poor sense to do this. Did you know that this condition is caused by a living fungus in your toenails? Take solace in knowing you are providing safe harbor for one of God's small creatures.

Saggy folds in flesh above the knee. When was the last time someone complimented your knees? No one cares about your knees. If your ass is holding up and your breasts are still above your navel, you have no place carping about your knees.

Loose, flappy skin on underside of forearm. You probably haven't noticed this one. Look in the mirror while crossing your arms. See what I'm talking about? Remember, until ten seconds ago, you didn't care about this. Why care now?

Unwanted hairs. Georgia O'Keeffe had visible wiry chin hairs, but no one remembers her for this. They remember her for large, vaginal nature paintings. Let this be an inspiration.

Vertical wrinkles radiating from upper lip. Don't trouble yourself over these, because soon there will be large heavy folds on either side of your mouth, and when this happens, you'll give anything to go back to the days when you only worried about upper lip lines. And you know what? You're living those glorious halcyon days right now!

Heavy, dark under-eye circles. Many athletes apply black greasepaint to this area to reduce glare and improve their game. You don't ever have to do this. That's a savings right there.

Skin tags. If you look through a dermatology textbook, you'll see that some people have even uglier things growing out of their skin. I heard somewhere that they don't necessarily all get bigger and bigger.

Gray hairs. Hairs coarsen and crook when they go gray. While some people feel that the frazzled, even witchlike appearance of gray hair is unattractive, those of you who have lived your whole life with thin, limp, Tom Petty hair will probably enjoy the added body.

Bulldog jowls. Don't let heavy jowls get you down. You know why? Because then you won't smile, and when you smile, no one can tell you have jowls.

Creases in front of ears. Police investigators use these to gauge perpetrators' ages in cases where it's hard to tell. Think of them like fingerprints. They make you you. Though if you've got neck cords, receding gums, skin tags, and bulldog jowls, God knows no one needs ear creases to tell your age.

I hope that you feel better now.

To Be (Too) Real: The Unexpected Consequences of Living an Authentic Life

Meredith Maran

I spent a month in France last summer. I know what you're thinking: the same thing everyone thought when they heard where I was going. Like so many other things in my big, fat, wonderful life, my summer plan sounded like one thing. And it was that. And it was also quite another.

"Paris in July! You're so lucky," everyone said. And they were right. And they were wrong.

I'm lucky—beyond lucky; there are no words for how far beyond lucky—to have been married, these last seven years, to a luscious, brilliant, loving, now-you-got-me-started French woman: my reason for making the trip. Lucky to have accrued sufficient frequent flier miles in the course of several previous trips, with the aforementioned wonderful wife, to cover the ticket. Lucky to be a freelance writer, so I could disappear for a month without putting in for vacation time (the best—in fact, the only—benefit of *having* no paid vacation time).

Did I mention that there's more to the story? For starters, I wasn't going to Paris. *Au contraire:* our pied-a-terror was in La Plaine St. Denis, a vibrant, fascinating, third-world Parisian "suburb" (French for "ghetto") one kilometer beyond the last Metro stop, in whose ancient, thick-walled buildings and narrow, garbage-strewn streets Tunisian and Senegalese and Pakistani immigrants live and raise their dashiki'ed, djalaba'ed, and Nike-T-shirt-ed children in cacophonous, shared-bathroom poverty. La Plaine is to Paris as Bedford-Stuyvesant is to Manhattan, as the Ida B. Wells projects are to Chicago, as Compton is to L.A.—you get the picture—but with better architecture and worse (in many cases, no) plumbing.

Contrary to popular opinion, I wasn't going to France to nibble baguette and brie in the Bois de Boulogne, or to lounge languidly beside the Loire. No, I was going in service to the domestic partner of my dreams, with whom I fell and remain in love in part because she is so *not* some boring, bourgeois Fruppie, no Sixth Arrondissement snob, but a put-your-multiculti-loving-money-where-your-mouth-is, community-organizing activist not entirely unlike *moi,* only more so—characteristics Katrine had manifested, long before I seduced and snatched her from her native land, by purchasing a 350-square-foot, two-and-a-half-room, no-bathroom-door, ground-floor apartment on what her outraged *papa* heartlessly, if only slightly inaccurately, called "the single worst street in Paris." Having lost her latest tenants, Katrine (and I, her yet-unlawfully-married wife) faced the task of inspecting and repairing whatever damage had been done to her *très petite maison* by a long series of renters. This accomplished, we would then need to rent it again.

Sparing you the unpleasant details, of which there were *beaucoup,* I will say only that in short order I'd learned the French (and in some cases, Wolof, Urdu, or Arabic) words for many, many invectives as well as the proper translations of "mildew," "cold shower," "extra-strength bleach," "heat wave," "emergency plumber," and whole phrases including, "They took the fridge, stove, and sink with them when they left," "Quiet down out there—it's 3 A.M.," and, "We're not renting out this hell hole. We're selling it—*maintenant.*" Between romantic interludes of ceiling/wall/floor-scouring, connubial cold-water dishwashing, and intimacy-building liaisons with a string of Parisian realtors—each of whom took the one-minute house tour with briefcase clutched to chest and upper lip curled in disdain, muttering the same one word, *particulier,* to describe the sort of person who might be convinced to take our beloved chateau off our hands—I took breaks to read the daily e-mails from my friends, family, editor, publicist, and agent, all begging enviously for details of my "Paris vacation."

On our last night there Katrine and I scrubbed ourselves down, dressed ourselves up, emptied the car of valuables (greatest among them our hardbound book of Paris street maps, which we'd used, in four weeks, exactly twice), parked beneath the brightest street light at the St. Denis train station, said a prayer to the French gods of car break-ins, and took the RER into Paris to meet a writer friend, Maddie, who was visiting from New York. As we emerged from underground at St. Germain des Prés, I went slack-jawed with wonder, as if I'd landed, suddenly, in a parallel universe. Mercedeses jousted with taxis on wide, landscaped boulevards; patisseries exuded intoxicating essences of *chocolat* and *beurre*; window-shopping matrons clicked along in Clergerie and Chanel, speaking, of all things, French. At last! I thought. My Paris vacation.

A stiffly uniformed doorman bowed us into the lobby of Maddie's Seventh Arrondissement *pension*. The concierge announced us, and we dropped into downy, velvet couches to wait. Beyond the lobby, on an ivy-draped patio a fountain tinkled gaily; tuxedoed wait-ers dipped and wove between chatting groups of stylish tourists, proffering espressos in tiny porcelain cups. "Bob's company is pay-ing," Maddie explained—apologized, really; her stockbroker husband embarrassed, as well as underwrote, her—as she, Katrine, and I exchanged hugs. Maddie led us up a curved flight of thickly carpeted stairs to her room. The foyer was the size of our apartment. The marble-and-gold bathroom featured, incredibly, not only a bath-tub but a door. The walls were embellished with molding, not mold; the bedroom floor was littered with discarded tissue paper and shop-ping bags, their logos a parade of high-fashion fantasies. Maddie went to freshen her lipstick. I sank to the polished parquet floor, slumped against the king-sized damask-dressed bed.

"I want this," I cried, from the bottom of my cold-shower-chilled heart. I seized an empty Gaultier bag, pressed my face against its thick, slick veneer. "I want this," I repeated more fervently still.

"So marry a stock broker," Katrine replied calmly. "Or stop writing books about teenagers and race and start writing about lavender fields in Provence."

This wasn't the first time my lovely bride and I had had this interchange, in one form or another. Even in my fevered state I realized it was not likely the last.

"I *can't*," I whined.

"You mean you won't," Katrine corrected me.

"Oh, why can't I have my politics," I moaned, "and a hot bath too?"

Those damn politics of mine: they stick to me like crazy glue; they plague me like a swarm of tsetse flies; they drive me like a ruthless boss. When all around me people were losing their politics and blaming it on their mortgages, those old sixties values clung to me like a poorboy sweater. When all around me activists were becoming—or marrying—lawyers and MBAs, moving to all-white neighborhoods, sending their kids to private schools, I was becoming more unemployable by the year, moving to a gritty Oakland neighborhood, sending my kids to gritty Oakland public schools, still hoarsely chanting, "The personal is political," a choir of one. When all around me writers were buying Tuscan villas, then enjoying protracted stays on the *Times* list with books about their oh-so-challenging but ultimately charming renovations, I kept writing books about the differences between how things are supposed to be in these United States and how they actually are, remaining doggedly attached to the notion—increasingly unpopular, as my royalty statements would soon show—that books were meant to change, not pretty up, the world.

I blame it all on my childhood—my adolescence, that is. I was raised by wolves: rescued from my parents' middle-class, middle-of-the-road wasteland by the prowling pack of cool kids who roamed the hallways of my prestigious New York high school. These countercultural missionaries, these do-right Dr. Doolittles, these sixties Svengalis, turned my life on a dime by introducing me to sex, drugs, rock and roll, and the breathtaking notion that a life could be—not to put too much of a nineties spin on it—*meaningful.*

Bye-bye Upper East Side, hello Avenue D. At age fifteen the soundtrack of my life switched from the Ronettes to a compilation album of Janis Joplin ("You know you got it/If it makes you feel good"), Marvin Gaye ("Picket lines and picket signs/Don't punish me with brutality"), and Jefferson Airplane ("Got to revolution"). Expelled from my graduation ceremony for passing out black armbands emblazoned with peace signs, which a few hundred graduates-to-be (or, in my case, -not-to-be) then raised aloft, fists clenched, as the mayor of New York began his commencement address; arrested soon thereafter for tossing a roach out the window of a *very* moving vehicle; recruited to the staff of an underground SDS newspaper while my classmates were being recruited to MIT and Yale, I was set, in those formative years, on a path that has not yet brought me to a crossroads tempting enough to take.

Thirty-five years later, with two sons old enough (but not, sadly, considerate enough) to have made me a grandmother, and the wrinkles to prove it, I'm still cruising down the revolution highway without any brakes. I've chosen for my friends and lovers marching-mates, not career-boosters; I schmooze but don't network. I've loved and married men; I've loved and married women, though not necessarily in that or any particular order. I've taken jobs, but not kept them. I've had thus far—and I hope the adventure is not much beyond half over—as I've said, a big, fat, wonderful life.

And yet. And still. Lest I appear to be bragging, well, as I've said, there's the other side of the story: my hellish trip to St. Denis masquerading as a Paris vacation, my virtuous values trumped by cravings for chic hotel rooms and couture. My choices, admirable or ridiculous as they may seem, have had consequences I would not have chosen (chronic financial uncertainty; a cranky, money-gulping hundred-year-old house; the cheapest medical insurance for myself and my kids—all less fun at fifty than they were at twenty-five) and consequences, at times, that I could barely stand. Paramount among them: the terrifying adolescence of my younger son. Sensitive by nature, possessing, as his third-grade teacher said, "the strongest sense of justice and injustice I've ever seen in so young a child," Jesse sank like a stone into the quicksand of the ghetto street life that beckoned so enticingly from just outside our front door. While my former comrades were taking corporate diversity workshops, writing checks to Greenpeace, and hiring SAT tutors to ensure their progeny's place in the sun, I was the one white mom in the visiting room at Juvenile Hall, the locally best-selling author juggling book tours with Jesse's court appearances, the freelance journalist chewing through her savings to pay the therapists, bail bondsmen, and lawyers who would, I prayed, save my son from the collision course with prison (or worse) upon which those politics of mine seemed to have placed him.

Jesse survived. Today, he thrives. Surprisingly to many (but not to me), he has been, since age twenty, the youngest and the only white preacher at Berkeley Mt. Zion Baptist church. He spends his days counseling teenagers in rehab, his nights doing prison ministry at the Juvenile Halls and jails where he once sat on the lockup side of the glass. Jesse's life goal, he says publicly and often, is to "comfort the afflicted and afflict the comfortable," words I might accurately use to describe my own. My older son, Peter, a recent no-armband-graduate of UC Berkeley (which he was actually paid to attend, so impressed were the financial aid auditors with the paucity of his mother's income), is going about the business of earning the title "photographer," crashing on his cousin's Los Angeles couch, documenting the intersection of art and politics called hip-hop.

A mother never stops worrying, of course, but on this one count I am confident: both Jesse and Peter now have, and are likely to continue having, big, fat, wonderful lives of their own. Despite the trials and traumas that my life choices have inflicted upon theirs, despite the disparities of culture, gender, spiritual practice, sexual orientation, and age that divide us, Peter and Jesse both show unmistakable signs of having inherited, absorbed, and/or—dare I say it?—embraced those damn values of their mother's. Thereby proving—what? This much, at least: that the politics and values dismissed by so many as "that old sixties stuff" are following another generation into the future, albeit enhanced with twenty-first-century sensibilities.

A couple of book tours ago, when it looked for a moment as though wealth were about to be bestowed upon us, Katrine and I composed what we named the "P-O" (Post-Oprah) list, which included such items as a hot tub for the backyard, a new car for one or both of us, a straw bale country cottage. Secretly, I added another item, my own private P-O fantasy. I dreamed of waving a glittering wand over my wife's hardworking head, pronouncing her "put out to pasture," setting her free from the travails of her landscaping business so that she could spend her days doing only what she loves to do. A phone call came; the moment passed. Oprah waved her wand over some other author's head; the show and the wealth went on without me. We tucked the list and our P-O dreams away.

Will it surprise you to learn that not once since then has Katrine turned to me nor I to Katrine and expressed a longing for a single item on that list? Not to put too sixties a spin on it, but it seems to be enough for us, reveling daily in the great good fortune of our love. To my own list of "N-O" (Non-Oprah) blessings I would, today, add these: the great good fortune of mothering two sons who are sure to— again, forgive the archaic invocation—leave the world a better place than they found it. The great good fortune of friends and family who cheer me along on my path, ruts and all. And the great good fortune of waking up nearly every morning wanting to do whatever it is that my big, fat life has in store for me that day.

Call me old-fashioned, downwardly mobile, a victim or a relic of the past. I'll take the cold showers and the working vacations. I'll trade the good life for a life that stands a chance of actually doing some good. I'm keeping those damn politics because they shaped, spurred, and saved me, and because I still believe they might do that for the world as well. And so. And still. *Je ne regrette rien.*

Heroin/e

Cheryl Strayed

When my mother died, I stripped her naked. Plush round belly and her pale breasts rising above. Her arms were black-and-blue from all the needles going in. Needles with clear liquid and needles that only the nurses had a hold of and other needles gripping constantly into her, held tight with tape to the translucent skin of her hand or the silk skin of her wrist. And not one of those needles trying to save her. I picked her dead hand up. It did not want to be held. Her skin was dry and cracked and stabbed. When she died, the nurse took the needle out forever. But I wanted it back, and eventually I would get it.

The day they told us my mother had cancer I was wearing green. Green pants, green shirt, green bow in my hair. My mother had sewn this outfit for me. I didn't like such a themed look, but I wore it anyway, to the Mayo Clinic, as a penance, an offering, a talisman. We found a vacant wheelchair and I got into it and raced and spun down the hallway. Cancer, at this point, was something we did not have to take seriously. My mother was forty-five. She looked fine, beautiful, I would later think, *alive*. It was just the two of us, me and mother. There were others too, my stepfather working his job, wondering, my grandparents waiting by the phone, wanting to know if it was true, if perhaps the oncologist in Duluth had been mistaken after all. But now, as before, as it would always be, it was only me and my mother.

In the elevator she sat in the wheelchair and reached out to tug at my pants. She rubbed the fabric between her fingers proprietarily. "Perfect," she said.

I was twenty-two. I believed that if a doctor told you that you were going to die soon, you'd be taken to a room with a gleaming wooden desk. This was not so. My mother sat with her shirt off on top of a table with paper stretched over it. When she moved, the room was on fire with the paper ripping and crinkling beneath her. She wore a pale yellow smock with strings meant to be tied. I could see her soft back, the small shelf of flesh that curved down at her waist. The doctor said she'd be lucky if she lived a year. My mother blinked her wet eyes but did not cry. She sat with her hands folded tightly together and her ankles hooked one to the other. Shackled to herself. She'd asked the doctor if she could continue riding her horse. He then took a pencil in his hand and stood it upright on the edge of the sink and tapped it down on the surface hard. "This is your spine after radiation," he said. "One jolt and your bones will crumble like a dry cracker."

First we went to the women's restroom. Each of us locked in separate stalls, weeping. We didn't say a word. Not because we felt so alone in our grief, but because we were so together in it, as if we were one body instead of two. I could feel her weight leaning against the door, her hands slapping slowly against it, causing the entire frame of the bathroom stalls to shake. Later we came out to wash our hands and faces, standing side by side in the ladies' room mirror.

We were sent to the pharmacy to wait. I sat next to my mother in my green pantsuit. There was a big bald boy in an old man's lap. There was a woman who had an arm that swung wildly from the elbow. She held it stiffly with the other hand, trying to calm it. She waited. We waited. There was a beautiful dark-haired woman who sat in a wheelchair. She wore a purple hat and a handful of diamond rings. We could not take our eyes off her. She spoke in Spanish to the people gathered around her, her family and perhaps her husband. "Do you think she has cancer?" my mother whispered loudly to me. There was a song coming quietly over the speakers. A song without words, but my mother knew the words anyway and sang them softly to herself. "Paper roses, paper roses, oh they're only paper roses to me," she sang. She put her hand on mine and said, "I used to listen to that song when I was young. It's funny to think of that. To think about listening to the same song now. I would've never known." My mother's name was called then: her prescriptions were ready. "Go get them for me," she said. "Tell them who you are. Tell them you're my daughter."

My mother said I could have her jewelry box. She said, "When I am done with it." She was lying on the bed that my stepfather had made for her, for them, with branches twisting and arching up behind her, leaves and jumping bugs carved discreetly into them. There was a dancing pink girl who lived in the jewelry box. She stood and twirled around to the song that played when you wound it up and opened the box. The song changed as it slowed, became sorrowful and destitute. The girl tottered and then stopped as if it hurt her. She had lips the size of a pinhead painted red and a scratchy pink tutu. When we shut the box she went down into it, stiff as a board, bending at the feet. "I always wonder what the ballerina is thinking," my mother said dreamily.

When my mother got cancer I'd folded my life down. I was a senior in college in Minneapolis, and I'd convinced my professors to allow me to be in class only two days each week. As soon as those days were over, I drove north to the house in rural Minnesota where I'd grown up, racing home, to my mother. I could not bear to be away from her. Plus, I was needed. My stepfather was with my mother when he could be, when he wasn't working as a carpenter in an attempt to pay the bills. I cooked food that my mother tried to eat. She'd say: pork chops and stuffed green peppers, cherry cheesecake and chicken with rice, and then holler the recipes out to me from her bed. When I'd finished she'd sit like a prisoner staring down at her steaming plate. "It smells good," she'd say. "I think I'll be able to eat it later." I scrubbed the floors. I took everything from the cupboards and put new paper down. My mother slept and moaned and counted and swallowed her pills, or on good days she sat in a chair and talked to me, she paged through books.

"Put these on for me." My mother sat up and reached for a pair of socks. It had been only a few weeks since we'd learned of her cancer, but already she could not reach her own feet without great pain. I bent at her feet. She held the ball of socks in her hand. "Here," she said. I had never put socks onto another person, and it was harder than you might think. They don't slide over the skin. They go on crooked and you have to work to get them on right. I became frustrated with my mother, as if she were holding her foot in a way that made it impossible for me. She sat back with her body leaning on her hands on the bed, her eyes closed. I could hear her breathing deeply, slowly. "God dammit," I said. "Help me." My mother looked down at me, silently.

We didn't know it then, but this would be the last time she was home. Her movements were slow and thick as she put her coat on, and she held onto the walls and edges of doors as she made her way out of the house. On the drive to the hospital in Duluth she looked out the window. She said, "Look at the snow there on those pines." She told me to toot my horn when I went past Cindy's house in Moose Lake. She said, "Be careful of the ice. It's black ice." She held an old plastic milk jug with the top cut off so she could vomit into it during the drive. My mother put one hand up to her ribs, where the cancer lived, and pressed gently. "Wouldn't that be something, to get into an accident now?"

Three years after my mother died I fell in love with a man who had electric blue hair. I'd gone to Portland, Oregon, to visit a friend, seeking respite from the shambles my life had become. I had thought that by then I'd have recovered from the loss of my mother and also that the single act of her death would constitute the only loss. It is perhaps the greatest misperception of the death of a loved one: that it will end there, that death itself will be the largest blow. No one told me that in the wake of that grief other griefs would ensue. I had recently separated from the husband I loved. My stepfather was no longer a father to me. I was alone in the world and acutely aware of that. I went to Portland for a break.

I'll call the man with electric blue hair Joe. I met him on his twenty-fourth birthday and drank sangria with him. In the morning he wanted to know if I'd like some heroin. He lived on a street called Mississippi, in North Portland. There was a whole gathering of people who'd rigged up apartments above what had been a thriving Rexall drugstore. Within days I lived there with him. In the beginning, for about a week, we smoked it. We made smooth pipes out of aluminum foil and sucked the smoke of burning black tar heroin up into them. "This is called chasing the dragon!" Joe said, and clapped his hands. The first time I smoked heroin it was a hot sunny day in July. I got down on my knees in front of Joe, where he sat on the couch. "More," I said, and laughed like a child. "More, more, more," I chanted. I had never cared much for drugs. I'd experimented with each kind once or twice, and I drank alcohol with moderation and reserve. Heroin was different. I loved it. It was the first thing that worked. It took away every scrap of hurt that I had inside of me. When I think of heroin now, it is like remembering a person I met and loved intensely. A person I know I must live without.

The first time they offered my mother morphine, she said no. "Morphine is what they give to dying people," she said. "Morphine means there's no hope."

We were in the hospital in Duluth. We could not get the pillows right. My mother cried in pain and frustration when the nurses came into the room. The doctor told her that she shouldn't hold out any longer, that he had to give her morphine. He told her that she was *actively dying*. He was young, perhaps thirty. He stood next to my mother, a gentle hairy hand slung into his pocket, looking down at her in the bed.

The nurses came one by one and gave her the morphine with a needle. Within a couple of weeks my mother was dead. In those weeks she couldn't get enough of the drug. She wanted more morphine, more often. The nurses liked to give her as little as they could.

One of the nurses was a man, and I could see his penis through his tight white nurse's trousers. I wanted desperately to pull him into the small bathroom beyond the foot of my mother's bed and offer myself up to him, to do anything at all if he would help us. And also I wanted to take pleasure from him, to feel the weight of his body against me, to feel his mouth in my hair and hear him say my name to me over and over again, to force him to acknowledge me, to make this matter to him, to crush his heart with mercy for us. I held my closed book in my hand and watched him walk softly into the room in his padded white shoes. My mother asked him for more morphine. She asked for it in a way that I have never heard anyone ask for anything. A mad dog. He did not look at her when she asked him this, but at his wristwatch. He held the same expression on his face regardless of the answer. Sometimes he gave it to her without a word, and sometimes he told her no in a voice as soft as his shoes and his penis in his pants. My mother begged and whimpered then. She cried and her tears fell in the wrong direction, not down over the lush light of her cheeks to the corners of her mouth but away from the edges of her eyes to her ears and into the nest of her hair on the bed.

I wanted it and I got it, and the more heroin we got, the stingier we became with it. Perhaps if we snorted it, we thought, we'd get higher on less. And then, of course, the needle. The hypodermic needle, I'd read, was the barrier that kept the masses from heroin. The opposite was true with me. I loved the clean smell of it, the tight clench around my arm, the stab of hurt, the dull badge of ache. It made me think of my mother. It made me think of her, and then that thought would go away into the loveliest bliss. A bliss I had not imagined.

There was a man named Santos whom we called when we wanted heroin. He would make us wait by the telephone for hours, and then he'd call and instruct us to meet him in the parking lot of a Safeway. I sat in the car while Joe took a short drive with Santos in his yellow Pinto, and then Joe would calmly get back into the car with me and we'd go home. On some occasions we went to Santos' house.

Once he sat in his front window with a shotgun across his lap. Once he clutched my thigh when Joe left the room and told me that if I came to see him alone he'd give me heroin free. Another time he held his baby daughter, just a month old. I looked at her and smiled and told Santos how beautiful she was, and inside of me I felt the presence of my real life. The woman who I actually was. The kind of woman who knows the beauty of a baby, who will have a baby, who once was a baby.

The days of my mother's death, the morphine days, and those that followed, the heroin days, lasted only weeks, months—but each day was an eternity, one stacked up on the other, a cold clarity inside of a deep haze. And unoccupied as well. Just me and my mother, or the ghost of her, though others surely came and went.

Some days flowers came to my mother's hospital room, and I set them on the edges of tables and windowsills. Women came too. Women who volunteered for the hospital. Old Catholic women, with hair cut close to the scalp or woven into long braids and pinned to their heads. My mother greeted them as she did the flowers: impervious, unmoved, resolute.

The women thought it would be for the best when my mother died. They sat next to me on the vinyl furniture and told me in low tones about the deaths of their own mothers. Mothers who had died standing at kitchen sinks, in the back seats of cars, in beds lit with candles. And also about the ones who made it. The ones with the will to live. Of tumors vanishing and clean blood and opaque bones. People who fought it, who refused to die. The ones who went and then came back. The survivors. The heroes. The heroines. It would be for the best, they whispered, when it was over. Her life, that is. My mother's.

People whom I knew came, and I did not recognize them at first. It seemed they all wore strange hats or other disguises during this time, though I'm certain that is not true. They were friends of my mother's. They couldn't bear to stay in the room, so instead they left chicken potpies and bread. Scalloped potatoes and blocks of cheddar cheese. By then my mother couldn't eat half a banana. Couldn't lick a lick of a Popsicle without retching it back up. They said her name to her, and she said their names back to them, hoarse and confused. She said, "How nice you came." And she put a wan smile on her face. Her hair was flattened against her head, and I reached to smooth it into place.

I asked my mother if she would like for me to read to her. I had two books: *The Awakening* by Kate Chopin and *The Optimist's Daughter* by Eudora Welty. These were books we'd read before, books we'd loved. So I started in, but I could not go on. Each word I said erased itself in the air. It was the same when I tried to pray. I prayed fervently, rabidly, to God, any god, to a god I could not identify or find. I prayed to the whole wide universe and thought perhaps God would be in it. I prayed and I faltered. God, I realized, had no intention of making things happen or not, of saving my mother's life. God would come later, perhaps, to help me bear it.

She taught me to knit, my mother, and I did this in the room while she slept and lived the last while. It occurred to me that she had taught me to knit for this particular occasion. So that I would have a place to put my hands and my eyes. "What are you making?" she asked.

"A scarf."

"For who?" Her hand pinched the sheet that covered her

"I don't know," I said. "I'm simply knitting a scarf." The best part about knitting is the tapping, tapping, tapping of the needles. A sound so silent it is like the language of snakes or rabbits or deer.

Eventually the nurses and doctors stopped paying any mind to what my mother said or wanted. They looked to me to decide how much morphine to give her. They said I had a choice: she could be in great pain but fairly conscious, or she could be comfortable but higher than a kite, and usually passed out. Ultimately, it was not up to me. "Promise me one thing," she said. My mother was not dramatic or concise in her dying. She hadn't offered a single directive in the past days, and I was desperate for guidance. "That you won't allow me to be in pain anymore. I've had too much pain."

"Yes," I said, "yes."

There was using heroin and also not using it. In the mornings when I woke, groggy and drained, I'd stand in front of the mirror and talk to myself. I was shocked by my own life. This was not meant to be, I'd think in the mornings. Stop it, I said. No more. And then I would shower and dress and take a bus downtown to serve people coffee and pancakes. At two in the afternoon I'd take the bus home again with hopefully sixty bucks in my pocket for another score of heroin. This is how it went.

Joe waited for me to get home. He cooked me macaroni and cheese and called Santos. He pulled me into his bed and jumped up when the phone rang. I made him stick the needle into me the first time, and then he taught me how to do it myself. What I loved about Joe is that he didn't love me, or himself. I loved that he would not only let me but help me destroy myself. I'd never shared that with another person. The dark glory of our united self-destruction had the force of something like love. I get to do this, I thought. I get to waste my life. I felt a terrible power within me. The power of controlling the uncontrollable. Oh, I thought, I get to be junk.

But this was not meant to be. My husband, Mark, called me. He was in town and wanted to see me. The friend I'd come to visit in Portland had told him about Joe and about my using heroin, and in response he drove from Minneapolis to talk to me. I met him within the hour at our friend's house. He sat at the table in the kitchen with the branches of a fig tree tapping on the window nearby. He said, "You look, you look . . . different. You seem so, how can I say this—you seem like you aren't here." First he put his hands on mine, and we held onto one another, locked hand to hand. I couldn't explain it to him, the why. And then we fought. He stood up and screamed at me so loudly that I put my hands over my head for cover. His arms gestured madly in the air, at nothing. He clawed at himself and ripped the shirt from his own back and threw it at me. He wanted me to go home with him in an hour. Not for a reunion but to get away, not from Joe but from heroin.

I told Mark I needed to think. I drove back to Joe's apartment and sat in a lawn chair he kept on the sidewalk. Heroin made me dumb, or distant, rather. A thought would form and then evaporate. I couldn't get a hold of my mind. I sat in the lawn chair on the sidewalk, and a man walked up to me and said his name was Tim. He took my hand and shook it and told me that I could trust him. He asked if I could give him three dollars for diapers, then if he could use my phone, and then if I had change for a five-dollar bill, and on and on in a series of twisting questions and sorry stories that confused and compelled me to stand and pull the last ten dollars I had out of my jeans pocket. He saw the money and took a knife out of his shirt. He held it gently to my chest and said, "Give me that money, sweetheart."

I packed a few things and called Mark. When he pulled up to the corner where I was waiting, I got into his car. By sunset Portland was long gone. In Montana we checked into a motel to sleep. I held myself in bed, rocking with a headache, a sickness in my gut. Mark brought me water and chocolate and watched television. I sat in the car as we drove across the country, and I felt my real life present but unattainable, as if heroin had taken me entirely from myself. Mark and I fought and cried and shook the car with our fighting. We were monstrous in our cruelty. We talked kindly afterward, shocked at ourselves and each other. We decided that we would get divorced. I hated him and I loved him. He had known my mother. I felt trapped, branded, held, and beloved. Like a daughter. "I didn't ask you to come to Portland," I screamed. "You came for your own reasons," I said.

"Maybe," he said.

"You love me that much?" I asked. "You came all this way to get me? Why?"

"Because," he said. "Just because."

I wanted my mother to love me, but more. I wanted her to prove it, to live. To go to battle and to win. And if she was going to die, I wanted her to tell me, in the end, how I should live, without her. Until that point I had wanted just the opposite. I could not bear for her to tell me what to do or how to live. I had wanted to be unknown by her, opaque to her wondering eyes.

The last days, my mother was not so much high as down under. When she woke, she'd say, "Oh, oh." Or she'd let out a sad gulp of air. She'd look at me, and there would be a flash of love. Other times she'd roll back into sleep as if I were not there. Sometimes when my mother woke she did not know where she was. She demanded an enchilada and then some applesauce. She'd say, "That horse darn near stepped on me," and look around the room for it accusingly. During this time I wanted my mother to say to me that I had been the best daughter in the world. I did not want to want this, but I did, inexplicably, as if I had a great fever that could only be cooled by those words. I went so far as to ask her directly, "Have I been the best daughter in the world?" She said yes, I had, of course. But this was not enough. I wanted those words to knit together in my mother's mind and for them to be delivered, fresh, to me. I was ravenous for love.

One day a woman with a clipboard asked if I'd go with her to the cafeteria. She said that she wanted to talk to me about a donation my mother had made. Her name was Janet and she was dressed in a navy-colored shirt with little white fringes on each shoulder, as if she were the captain of something. Her fingernails were long and red and they clicked together when she moved her hands in certain ways.

When we sat down with two cups of coffee between us, she told me that my mother was an organ donor but that because she had cancer throughout her body they would only take her eyes.

"Her eyes?"

"Well not the whole eye, of course, but parts of the organ." Janet took her cup up into her hands; one fingernail tapped against it. "We make it a policy to inform people close to the donor. In your mother's case, upon death, we will need to place ice on her eyes in order to preserve them." She thought about this for a moment. "This way you will understand what is happening when you see that we must put the bags of ice on her face. The removal is performed within a few hours after her death." Her fingernails went up to the sides of her face, hovering in midair. "Small incisions will be made at the side of each eye." Janet showed me this, pointing with her own sharp nails. "The skin will be sutured carefully to disguise signs of this procedure." She swallowed a sip of coffee and looked at me. "It does not preclude an open-casket viewing."

I dreamed of heroin. I woke in the middle of the night with a wanting so deep I was breathless. I had started seeing a therapist to talk about heroin. She told me that this wanting was normal, that indeed when you use heroin the brain responds by activating pleasure neurons that would normally remain dormant. She said it would take months for them to calm. Until then, they go on aching to be fed. Trying to trick your body into it. I could see them, spindly arms with mouths like flowers, blooming or wilting and them blooming again. "What about pain?" I asked her. "Are there neurons in the brain that come alive only with agony? And if so, how long does it take for them to die, to fold back into themselves and float away?"

I saw Joe two more times. I'd kept in touch with him; calling him late at night from Minneapolis, I could hear the heroin in his voice, making it soft and open. Within a month he was at my door. He looked weak and pale. He sat on my couch and shot up and then lurched into my kitchen and bent to vomit into the sink. He wiped his face and smiled. "It's worth it," he said, "getting sick. Because you feel so good through it all." We spent a week in my apartment using the supply of heroin he'd brought with him. I knew I had to end this, and finally I did. He left when I asked him to.

The second time I saw him, a year had passed and I was moving to Portland for reasons unrelated to him. We went to the beach for the day. He was no longer the smart, sexy, simpering man I'd fallen for, but a junkie. Joe had scabs on his skin from constant scratching; his bony arms were bruised and punctured. He didn't care anymore what color his hair was. I sat on the cool sand watching the Pacific

Ocean roar in while Joe locked himself in the public restroom to shoot up. I held myself stiff against the desire to join him. The ocean inched nearer and nearer to me with each passing minute. I was both sickened by Joe and compelled. I felt in the presence of a dying man, a young dying man, and I knew that I could never see him again if I wanted to live. And I did.

My mother didn't have time to get skinny. Her death was a relentless onward march. The hero's journey is one of return, but my mother's was all forward motion. She was altered but still fleshy when she died, the body of a woman among the living. She had her hair too, brown and brittle and frayed from being in bed for weeks.

From the room where she died I could see the great Lake Superior out her window. The biggest lake in the world, and the coldest. To see it, I had to work. I pressed my face sideways, hard, against the glass, and I'd catch a slice of it going on forever into the horizon. "A room with a view!" my mother exclaimed. "All of my life I've waited for a room with a view."

I arranged the flowers closer into my mother, to the edges of tables, so that she could see them without having to turn her head. Bouquets of pink carnations, yellow roses, daisies, and tiger lilies. Flowers that originated on other continents and were brought here to witness my mother's dying. She wanted to die sitting up, so I took all the pillows I could get my hands on and made a backrest for her. I wanted to take my mother and prop her in a field of yarrow to die. I covered her with a quilt that I had brought from home, one she had sewn herself out of pieces of our old clothing. "Get that out of here," she said savagely, and then kicked her legs like a swimmer to make it go away.

I watched my mother. It was March, and outside, the sun glinted off the sidewalks and the icy edges of the snow. It was Saint Patrick's Day and the nurses brought my mother a square block of green Jell-O that sat quivering on the table beside her. It was the last day of her life, and my mother did not sleep, she did not wake. She held her eyes still and open. They were the bluest thing in the room, perhaps in all of Duluth. Bluer than the lake. They were the color of the sky on the best day of your life.

My mother died fast but not all of a sudden. A slow-burning fire when flames disappear to smoke and then smoke to air. She never once closed her eyes. First they were bitter and then they were bewildered and then they changed again to something else, to a state that I have had, finally, to see as heroic. Blue, blue eyes. Daggers of blue wanting and wanting. To stay, to stay.

3.

Mind Over Matter

In our constant search for security we can never gain any peace of mind until we secure our own soul.

—Margaret Chase Smith

The Sick Girl

Gayle Brandeis

I had an orgasm during a proctoscopy when I was thirteen. At least that's what my doctor told me. I didn't feel a thing.

I did hear something as I stood against an upright screen, the scope working its way up my rectum. It sounded like when you squeeze the last bit of shampoo out of a plastic bottle, a flatulent splurt between my legs. When I pulled up my panties—which had been yanked down to my knees—there was a cold goopy mass on the cotton. It felt rotten against my skin.

"You had a little *moment* there, didn't you?" My doctor smirked, one eyebrow raised.

I hadn't felt any pleasure, but he was on to something. I never would have admitted this, but being sick was a turn-on for me. Not a physical turn-on. More of an emotional turn-on. Maybe even a spiritual turn-on. Perhaps that goop *was* orgasmic in an ectoplasmic kind of way. My sad little spirit getting its rocks off. My body doing what it could to keep me safe and small.

I had started to get sick earlier that year, beset with stomach pains and massive bouts of diarrhea. We were about to move from my childhood apartment in Evanston, Illinois, to a house in the tony suburb of Winnetka. It was a wrenching move for me. I loved that apartment. It was the only home I had ever known. I loved waking up each morning and looking out at Lake Michigan—that vast, seemingly endless expanse. It made me feel expansive myself. And now we were moving away, moving to a house that was across the street from a forest preserve. The trees were nice, but I knew they masked a nearby landfill. They couldn't mask the smell, though. The sweet rotten stench of garbage often wafted into our new yard.

I knew that I was moving away from my childhood, moving away from all that was pure and innocent, moving toward a messier, smellier future. I had no desire to grow up. I wanted to be a child forever; to play all day at the lakeshore, to live in a never-ending make-believe world with my sister, Elizabeth, to not have to worry about the scary, sweaty world of boys. The idea of my body growing, changing, appalled me. I knew from reading Judy Blume that those changes were painful and confusing, and I wanted to have nothing to do with them. I wanted to stay in my fast, free, wonderfully simple child body, the one that asked nothing of me but food and sleep and play. I wanted to stay a child who could fit on the laps of my parents, who would be forever in their care. When I was younger, I had informed my parents that I would never move any further than Apartment 5G across the hall. But now we were moving twenty miles away. I kissed each wall of 5B before they dragged me away.

It took a while for doctors to figure out what was wrong with me. At first they thought it was lactose intolerance. Then they thought it was irritable bowel syndrome. Finally, after a series of mortifying and uncomfortable tests, they diagnosed me with Crohn's disease, a chronic inflammatory bowel disease, sister to ulcerative colitis but usually located in the small intestine, although it can strike any part of the digestive tract, from mouth to anus. Mine seemed to settle into junctures—the place where the stomach met the small intestine, where the small intestine met the colon. That made sense. Transitions, junctures, were difficult for me.

I liked to think of the small intestine as the semicolon. It was my favorite punctuation mark. I was an indecisive girl—if you asked me which I preferred, the comma or the period, it would have been hard for me to choose. With the semicolon, though, I got the best of both worlds—the period and the comma, together forever. Plus, it bridged the gap between the two marks. The comma was slippery—an arcing fish you could never quite grasp; the period was so stark and final. The semicolon was somewhere in between—a deep breath, a held breath, a pause (as they say) that refreshes.

Being sick became the semicolon in the run-on sentence of my life. It offered a resting point between childhood and whatever was going to come afterward. A suspended state. A falling out of time. A limbo. A lapse. A chance to get my bearings before the next clause of my life began.

Being sick also became the central part of my identity. I spent much of my freshman year of high school in the hospital—having one test after another, being fed and medicated via IV so my intestines could "rest." I thus became a curiosity, an instant celebrity. If I hadn't gotten sick, I would have easily faded into invisibility. I was quiet and shy, plus my teeth were crooked and my chest (to my relief) was flat. But now I had become "the sick girl," which was as close to the "It girl" as I was ever going to get. I embraced this new notorious identity with relish, fell easily into its murky haze. While I was in the hospital, my class sent me flowers, cards, even a male belly dancer. When I returned to school, shaky and pale, they nominated me for student council and I won by a landslide. My teachers were kind, solicitous. I could leave the class any time I needed to run to the bathroom. I didn't even have to raise my hand. I was royalty. I was famous.

Eventually, after months of medicines that gave me a moon face and hairy arms and a constant taste of metal in my mouth, after months of being catered to and coddled and pitied, I started to feel better. This freaked me out. I wasn't ready to be a normal teenager, a healthy girl. There was nothing to gain, as far as I could see, by relinquishing my romantic status as a weak and languishing figure. My doctors were vaguely menacing, the procedures were painful and degrading, but their cloistered world seemed safe, somehow. Safer, certainly, than the life of a normal teenager, which seemed so dark and unknown, filled with chaos. I wasn't ready for that kind of free fall; I preferred the devil I knew.

So I did what I thought I had to. I took my life, my illness, into my own hands. When the diarrhea stopped, I took Ex-Lax to start it up again. When the pain went away, I became an actress, the diva of disease. This went on for almost a year. My period started and I didn't tell anyone; I knew it was a sign that I was getting healthy, that I was a normal teenage girl, and I didn't want anyone to see me that way. I made makeshift pads out of tissue paper and flushed them down the toilet; eventually clogging the pipes. When the plumber pulled out the disgusting mass, I feigned innocence along with the rest of the family. I went from one lie to another. I spent much of the summer in a wheelchair because I started limping after my doctors mentioned that the Prednisone I had been taking might cause bone damage. My brain was in a constant haze; it took a lot of work to maintain deception.

One night, my parents were hosting a business party at our house. My father owned a direct-mail marketing company, which, unbeknownst to me, was on the brink of bankruptcy. He was courting clients, trying to keep the family out of financial ruin. I didn't know anything about this; all I knew was that I didn't feel like talking to anyone. I pretended the pain was flaring up again. I had already taken a shower, but I put my nightgown back on and crawled back into bed. I could hear chattering and laughing downstairs, could smell wine and whiskey and perfume, and was thrilled to not have to be part of it. I hated talking to grown-ups. I hated talking, in general. Parties were the worst; I never knew what to say. Sometimes I fantasized about being deaf and mute so I would have to write all my words down on a chalkboard hanging around my neck. Writing was so much easier for me than using my physical voice.

A couple of guests insisted on seeing me, the poor brave sick girl, and my mother ushered them into my dimly lit room. One woman crouched beside my platform bed and touched my hair. It was still damp, and her hand recoiled. I was thrilled that she probably thought I was clammy with fever, not freshly shampooed.

One of the guests gave me a book: *Books from Writer to Reader*, signed by the author. I was known as a writer throughout my dad's company—his secretary, Doris, often typed up my handwritten stories and poems and had the pages laminated; coworkers read them before my dad brought them back home. I had my own little fan base there. I wondered if anyone could tell I was being author of my own illness, author of my own life. It was by far the best thing I had ever written.

The next chapter of my identity—my "inspirational sick girl" phase—soon followed. I created a board game, "The Road to a Healthy Digestive System." I became the youngest board member of the local chapter of the National Foundation for Ileitis and Colitis. I published my own newsletter, *The Gastrointestinal Gazette*, and wrote things like:

> I am hoping this paper will let you know you are not alone. Over 200,000 kids under the age of twenty have IBD, all of whom have to undergo the same symptoms, the same tests, and the same worries which you and I have. I have made it through, they have all made it through, and you will make it through too, if you just have the right attitude. The worst thing you can do is feel sorry for yourself. Of course a disease is a terrible thing to deal with, but you should not keep saying "Why me?" because you will live with it throughout your life, so you must learn to face facts.

I was not facing facts. Not at all. I got letters from people I had inspired, so I felt that I must be doing something right. My doctors were starting to see through the guise, though. When I showed my gastroenterologist my board game, he said, "You're spending way too much time thinking about this disease, Gayle. You need to focus on your real life."

I was shocked and insulted that he would say such a thing. The disease *was* my real life. The rest of my existence paled in comparison. It never occurred to me to look further than the diagnosis for a sense of self. I packed the game back up and held it close to my chest. How dare he insult my fabulous creation. It would get produced and I'd earn a million dollars and then he'd be sorry.

But I didn't earn a million dollars. And I was earning less and less sympathy. My sick-girl shtick was starting to grow old. The kids in my class had become accustomed to my Camille act; they barely paid attention anymore. My parents were so exhausted by schlepping me back and forth to the doctors' office, the hospital, so worn with worry, that I started to feel guilty. In a quest to get some of their attention, my younger sister, Elizabeth, started to act out; she had even run away. I had been so self-centered, I hadn't really thought about how my actions were affecting the rest of the family. In my obsession with my digestive tract, I hadn't realized that I had wedged my own head up my butt. I hadn't been able to see anything else. And I was starting to get claustrophobic.

Slowly, cautiously, I emerged from my sick-girl trance, taking tentative steps into being a teenager. I told my mom that my period had started (although I didn't tell her it had started over a year ago; I pretended it was my first ever). I started to let myself have fun. I began to date, and learned, to my surprise, that I enjoyed kissing boys. I began to spend more time with friends, doing silly teenage girl things—dyeing our hair green and blue, spinning around the room to Dead or Alive, feeling more and more alive with each crazy twirl.

As soon as I relinquished the sick-girl mantle, Elizabeth, who was twelve at the time, readily stepped into my old job. She began vomiting—projectile vomiting. It was like something from *The Exorcist*. We would be eating dinner; she would open her mouth and a huge firehouse of puke would spray across the table and splat against the wall. Quite impressive, it was. After watching me get all the attention for the past couple of years, it was her moment in the spotlight, her turn to shine.

Her doctors called it an eating disorder, and tried to treat it as such. My mother, who had raged when my doctors insinuated there might be an emotional element to my illness, threatened to sue. She refused to see our illnesses as anything other than physical. My sister, who lost so much weight she almost died, acted indignant, too, but years later, she confessed to me that she had indeed been making herself throw up, fabricating illness from the start. That sick-girl mystique is a powerful one, a seductive one. My sister and I both flew into sickness like it was the promised land, like it was Nirvana. And in a twisted way it was—a surefire strategy to get attention, to gain control over our lives. In illness we found a way to transcend the normal world, become something other, become something special.

But what a relief it was to be healthy. To not have to see life through a lens of pain, real or playacted. I slowly learned to become more at home within my skin. I slowly learned to trust my own body. I spent a lot of time dancing, coming to appreciate the creativity of my joints and muscles, the glow that comes from using the body as a means of expression. I fell in love for the first time and began to understand how powerful and transformative pleasure can be.

When I began to experience genuine gastrointestinal problems again, as a college freshman, I didn't welcome the illness; I was enjoying my life too much to be sidelined. I found out that Crohn's had most likely been a misdiagnosis. What I had was acute intermittent porphyria, a rare metabolic disorder that can manifest itself in many ways. In my case, it showed up as digestive disorders, but porphyria also causes neurological problems, vampirism, werewolf syndrome, and purple urine. It is what made King George mad. It was a pretty cool and surreal thing to attach to my name, but I didn't dwell on it. I focused on getting better so I could get back to my writing, my dancing, my friends.

In my senior year of college, I had the opportunity to travel to Bali with a group from the Naropa Institute, the noted school of Tibetan Buddhism based in Colorado, to study Balinese music and dance. About a week after I arrived, I came down with a violent case of "Bali belly." The constant dash to the bathroom, the explosive diarrhea, felt all too familiar.

I shared a stone bungalow with three women—my roommate, Celia, was a healer; next door were Rebecca, an herbalist and former midwife, and Angela, a nurse. If I had to be sick in Bali, at least I was surrounded by the right people.

One day, when I was feeling feverish and fretful, Celia climbed inside the mosquito netting around my bed and knelt beside me. Light poured through the window cut into the stone wall, filling her curly hair with fire. The air was humid as a mouth. She put one hand flat on my stomach. I flinched.

"You're carrying a lot of pain in there," she said. Her British accent was an instant balm.

"I was sick as a teenager," I told her, blinking back tears. I watched a lizard climb through the window, skitter across the wall. "I spent a lot of time in the hospital."

"For what?" she asked. I could feel heat pour from her hand, through my shirt, through my skin.

I told her about the Crohn's disease, the porphyria. I didn't tell her about pretending to be sick. I hadn't told anyone yet—not my sister, not my parents, not my boyfriend with whom I had been living for the last year and a half. It was my deepest, darkest secret.

"You have a lot to release," Celia said. I really started crying then, but she continued, her voice as calm as ever. "I know you'll probably want to have a baby some day, and you won't want to have so much negative energy stored up in your belly. The baby wouldn't like that."

I nodded, sniffling. My period was a week late at that point, but I hadn't said anything, hadn't been ready to confront my own suspicions.

"I'm going to lift my hand," she said. "And I want all the bad stuff in your belly to lift up with it. You don't need it anymore. Let it go and trust in your body's ability to heal itself."

I closed my eyes. I felt her hand rise from my stomach. My diaphragm bounced like a trampoline. I felt a space open near my solar plexus. I felt the pain and shame of those earlier years begin to dribble out, then stream, then shoot into the monsoonal air like a sprinkler, a geyser, a fine gray spray.

About a week later, I found out I was pregnant. This was not a planned event. My boyfriend and I had gotten engaged a few months before, but we weren't planning to start a family for several years. Now suddenly here I was, twenty-one and pregnant. And, much to my surprise, it felt right. I flew home so I could be with Matt and make some decisions. And I felt joy grow in my belly. My belly that had been the site, the source, of so much negativity, was now the source of new life, new light. And I welcomed it with all my heart, even more energetically than I had welcomed my illness years before. Over the next nine months, as I watched my belly balloon into something healthy and radiant, I watched myself blossom, too. I was a woman. A woman in the next clause of my life, the part of the sentence that followed the semicolon. A healthy, grown-up woman. And I knew I'd never be that sick girl again.

Heroes of the House

Louise Rafkin

But I cannot recount or name them all:
the many wives and daughters of the brave.

—The Odyssey

Once I decided to do it, my foray into professional housecleaning happened quickly. It was on the very day that I pinned my cleaning flyer on the supermarket bulletin board next to the offers of free kitties that the blinking light on my answering machine presented the reality of my newfound profession. A gynecologist and his wife wanted an estimate.

The four-bedroom tri-level Cape Cod summer home was dusted with a yellow coat of spring pollen. Trailing the woman, I scrutinized the bathrooms and counted the bedrooms. I figured and calculated. Then I choked. I blew the estimate, offering my speed-demon skills at a price that I rightly figured would land me the job. As it turned out, I cleaned that home for an entire summer for about what her husband would charge for a single Pap smear.

During my first few years I made a lot of mistakes. Times were lean. I said yes when I should have said no. I cleaned for people with dogs. I cleaned for people with gaggles of kids, even babies. Actually, babies are fine. It's only after they try feeding themselves that the trouble begins. I developed this equation: If there's a toddler, there has to be a dog—the dog will surely shed but at least the food on the floor will be taken care of.

That first year I took on a woman who paid me in loose change and talked me down five dollars on my quoted price for the job, this while I stood in her new million-dollar summer home. I worked for a couple who routinely scheduled huge parties the night *before* I came to clean.

But I accepted my Cinderella role dutifully and without complaint. During most of my early years on the job, I was a wimp.

"Where's that damn prince?" I complained to my coworker A.J. one day as we were leaving the house of the "Loose-Change Lady." (Most of the time I clean with A.J. or another coworker, who vacuums while I do the wet work—bathrooms and kitchens. It's important to have someone handy to complain to, plus, I prefer wet work. I enjoy spraying products meant to smell like the natural world—pine, citrus—yet still smell obviously like cleaning products.)

"I'm ready for that fairy-tale ending," I said to A.J. It had been a particularly bad day. Earlier, while I was on my hands and knees in the bathroom singing along with the song on my Walkman, Loose-Change Lady had tapped me on the shoulder. Signing wildly, she gesticulated that something was wrong. I moved my earphones aside and smiled wanly. She told me, "You're off-key."

"Fairy-tale ending?" A.J. challenged. "Cinderella ends up marrying some strange guy because of her shoe size and her sisters' evil eyes are pecked out by doves! They probably ended up freeloading on her the rest of their lives."

"You're right," I said. "She probably cleaned up after the whole lot of them—with her husband insisting she wear those uncomfortable glass slippers."

By accident, while reading a story to my niece, I discovered that despite his famous parentage, Hercules put in time as a cleaner. It was part of his penance for killing about six of his own kids.

As punishment, Hercules was given a set of tasks, one of which was to clean the Augean stables. They hadn't been cleaned for thirty years.

But Hercules didn't mess around with all that horseshit. He simply diverted two nearby rivers so that they ran smack through the stables.

Waves of horse manure swamped the flood plains, polluted endangered salmon-spawning grounds, and swept downstream into the backyards of some unsuspecting peons, but soon the job was finished. Apparently Hercules had better things to do than fret about the environment.

Although I was outraged by Hercules' selfish cleaning technique, my niece remained enamored with the macho hero. She did, however, come up with a sensible response to this fable: "Why *hadn't* those stables been cleaned for thirty years?"

Not surprisingly, there are few role models for responsible, strong-minded cleaners. As a kid I think I was only vaguely aware of a handful of prime-time TV cleaners. Beulah, the first black character to headline a TV show, and Hazel were the front-runners, living-in at the homes of wealthy white families. Later there was the wacky Alice who worked for the Brady Bunch, and the curmudgeonly Florence at the Jefferson's.

I never paid much attention to these characters. For the most part, they seemed silly and foolish. However, I did read and reread Peggy Parish's books about the simple-minded housekeeper Amelia Bedelia. When the overly literal Amelia was told to dress the chicken, she did just that, fashioning tiny clothes for the bird.

When I first began cleaning, I liked to think of myself as a somewhat hip and creative version of Amelia Bedelia. I could only pull this off for so long. Sooner or later, reality was bound to set in. My personal transformation from meek and mild scrubwoman to maid with a mind of her own occurred organically, but suddenly. It was several years into my cleaning life, at a house where the client had never even taken the time to learn my name. At the end of our shift, he'd hand me a check with the line for the name completely blank.

I was relocating a pair of his dirty underwear from the floor to a chair by means of a coat hanger. A.J. watched from across the bedroom, giggling.

"I don't move dirty underwear," I said to A.J.

"No?" she said, eyebrows up. "You could have fooled me."

Right then the man sailed in from the hall. "Change the sheets, would you?" Folded sheets in hand, he seemed baffled by my fishing maneuver.

"No," I said, the offending briefs dangling from the wire hook.

For the right person, I'd pick up dirty underwear, change sheets, and even sweep up dead rats (and I have), but this wasn't the right person.

"No," I said again, having made the decision that this was a job I no longer wanted. "We don't change sheets." Obviously angered, he tossed the bundle of sheets on the bed and left the room.

"Unless you want them really changed," I said to A.J. once he had departed. "Like shredded."

A.J. laughed, I laughed, and we never went back there again. It was my first good riddance, though I did see this guy years later in a movie theater. He was sitting in front of me, and I knew, if I didn't move, I could never enjoy the film. I was afraid I would be recognized.

And afraid I wouldn't be.

Although few can imagine them, there are fairy-tale moments in a housecleaner's life, despite crabby clients and sometimes being treated as less than human. I have felt flashes of transformation along the lines of Cinderella's, and witnessed situations as dramatic as Hercules' clean sweep.

One such moment involved a sweet elderly client. An alcoholic, he was almost always tipsy. One morning he met me at the door in a panic; he had somehow misplaced $1,000 in cash.

"Forget the cleaning," he told me. (I hated cleaning this house— it was large and rambling, and the only joy was finding bottles hidden in new places, like the guest shower.)

"Just find the money!" he implored, and I didn't dare get close to him. The smell, even at a distance, was overwhelming.

Together we turned the house upside down. Eventually, I discovered the money stuffed into an empty toilet-paper roll buried in the laundry hamper. With the wad of cash in my hand, I found him on the living room couch, weeping. Sighting the green roll, he jumped up, took my arm, and insisted on leading me in a celebratory waltz. At that moment, strange as it now seems, dancing together was the only thing we could have done.

I was tipped a crisp $100 and was home before noon.

At another house, I found my prince—of sorts. I was side-by-side at the sink with a client, a Hollywood somebody, who had taken years to warm to me. Whenever I was there, he was usually absorbed in his work, a splay of legal pads covered with scribbled bits of dialogue before him on the dining room table. Often he was on the phone talking to someone I've only experienced through the pages of *People* magazine. While cleaning, I'd listen in on his conversations, imagining what I thought would be a Somebody's life—palm trees and personal trainers.

Fastidious, he hated that his stainless-steel sink was stained. So one warm, sunny morning, I showed him the secret of sink de-rusting, and there we were, shoulder-to-shoulder, our elbows bumping, our muscles churning, swabbing the twin sinks.

He was amazed! Delighted! Rust stains, the great leveler. I imagined the advertisement: "Soft Scrub—even eradicates class distinctions!" And who could have thought that we, the two of us, from such different parts of the world, would share such a moment?

Often I just can't help myself. Once, while I was dusting at a one-time-only job, I found a letter taped onto the back of a picture frame. It was unsealed and addressed to a man I vaguely knew. Of course, I couldn't resist: I read a long confession of obsessive love from another man who had previously lived in this house but had long since left town. I couldn't imagine how the letter had come to be stuck to the back of the picture, or why it was there.

"I hope someone will send this," it closed. "I am not brave enough to accept my passion."

Later that day I mailed the letter. Sometimes I want my presence in a house to have an effect beyond that of a well-mopped floor.

Learning to Walk

Amy Krouse Rosenthal

The Mister and I were away at a spa in Tuscon called Miravel, a place whose logo includes the words "life in balance," which got me right there. The buzz at the spa was that something called Equine Experience was the class to take. Now I am not a horse person—I fell asleep during *The Horse Whisperer*, but everyone promised that while, yes, you basically groomed horses, it was much more, that you learned about yourself in a way you can't imagine. So, with great unenthusiasm, I signed up . . . then promptly blew it off the next morning when the time came. I almost escaped equineless, but on the eve of our departure, I collapsed under the pressure of the eighty-seventh person raving about it. So I signed up for the 9:00 A.M. class on our last day, knowing that that would leave me about four and one-half spare minutes before our noon pickup time. Which was good, 'cause I had had enough of this leisurely pace crap.

"I'm Wyatt," said a graying Marlboro-ish man. A couple of sentences later, it was clear that he was more of a Plato-ish man, with a dash of the Tootsie Pop wise old owl. I subsequently learned that Wyatt had dropped out of life for a good five years and basically read every book ever written. He had a few things to share.

Wyatt took the three of us, all women, to the ring. There was a large horse standing alongside the fence. Wyatt went into the center.

"Now I am going to get the horse to start walking." And with that, the horse started walking.

Keep in mind that words mean nothing to a horse; Wyatt was communicating solely through body language. He explained that the horse picks up on and basically mirrors back our energy, our intentions.

"Now the horse will trot." And the horse began to trot.

"Now he will run." And the horse ran.

Then Wyatt brought the horse back down to a trot, then a walk, then a stop. We three spectators were awestruck, giddy. It was really a beautiful and powerful thing to have witnessed.

"Your turn," he said.

Body language? Here's what my body language was saying: "Please, God, let me go last." So first one, then the other, woman took center ring and, with Wyatt's gentle guidance, figured out how to shift her energy and turn her body ever so slightly to take the horse from stop to run and back. Each had difficulty with one aspect or another—one couldn't get the horse to budge at first—but with Wyatt's coaching, everyone more or less mastered the exercise.

Wyatt's gaze fell my way. I said a silent prayer: *Please let me be able to do this, please let the horse not run me over—I still want to see the new Woody Allen movie.*

Wyatt showed me how to stand at a certain angle to the horse and how to adjust my wrist so the whip would dangle just so. And just like that, the horse started walking. Wow, no problem. Then he instructed me to think, "Trot," and turn ever so slightly. The horse started trotting. Cool. I'm really doing it. But then before Wyatt could okay the next level, and without my realizing what I had done, the horse was running. Running and running and running.

"Think trot," said Wyatt. And I tried to shift my energy back down and convey "Trot" to this frantic creature. The horse responded. He began running even faster, as if someone had laced his oats with a case of Dexatrim.

"All right, think walk, Amy. Walk. Walk. Walk," Wyatt said. I tried to think "Walk," to think slow; to be one with my loose, floppy shoulders, to think of taking a Sunday afternoon stroll while holding a bunny. But apparently my body language has a strong Chicago accent, because this horse was not understanding me one bit; he thought I was saying, "Run, freaky horse, run." After another minute or so—or maybe it was six days—of Wyatt's patient and pointed coaching, the horse finally, finally, finally settled into a trot, then a walk, then stopped.

Man.

I can say that at the time, this felt like one of the most profound lessons of my life, an image sure to make it into the final life-flashing-before-me slide show. I walked away with a clear agenda, a vow to mellow the hell out. Granted, within twenty minutes of being home, I blew all of that off. But I am able to catch myself now and again. I keep seeing the horse: running and running and running, and begging me to give him a break.

Walking the Labyrinth with Mother
In Memoriam: Min Kyung-Im
March 26, 1936 – July 20, 2001

Peggy Hong

Losing a father is like riding a bike without a helmet, a car without a seatbelt. For weeks after he died, I felt unsheathed and vulnerable. I'd wrap myself in scarves and hats. Coats and shawls, too, to protect my backside. When I rode my bike, I felt wobbly. A father is a tether to the earth; a father is grounding and stability. But losing a mother, losing the only mother you have, is losing touch. Pats, hugs, a casual hand stroking your hair. Even the long distance touch: early morning phone calls, packages wrapped in brown grocery bags with "Milwaukee" misspelled. Losing her touch even though I'd go months without seeing her, even though I lived in different parts of the country for most of my adult life. Although I have a husband and three children, close friends, and lots of opportunities for intimacy and human contact, no one treats me with the bodily familiarity my mother did. I could not have prepared for the shock of permanently losing her—her body, my first home, her familiar touch.

Mother came to live with us when she was sixty-five. She'd served my father as wife, mother of their three children, and householder, and she'd nursed him until his death; now he was gone.

Chronically ill herself, she could no longer live independently. After giving away all she could, Mother had sold her house in Western New York and moved into the first-floor flat of our duplex in Milwaukee, on the shores of Lake Michigan. For the first two months, she enjoyed unprecedented good health, walking to the lake, the grocery store, cafés. She found a Korean church and got involved at the senior center. Then she got sick.

Or rather, she'd always been sick; it just started to show up again. For over twenty years, Mother had been debilitated with myasthenia gravis, an autoimmune neurological disorder that results in progressive weakening of the muscles. She had a heart condition, a lung condition, you name it.

The afternoon she came home from the senior center field trip to the angel museum was when she collapsed in bed. My ten-year-old son, Malachi, was downstairs in her flat, playing games on her computer. He said he heard her whisper for water. Already she could hardly talk or move. Any responsible daughter would have immediately called an ambulance. But me, I'm a do-it-yourself kind of gal when it comes to medical matters, a woman who gave birth to my children at home because I so distrust doctors and hospitals. And my mom felt the same way. That's what happens when you come from a family of doctors, you know all too well the limitations of medicine and how incompetent doctors can be. My father and both grandfathers were doctors; my brother, an uncle, and several cousins followed in their footsteps. My parents hoped I would continue the lineage, but I managed to escape and study literature instead. Mother felt sure a doctor would be able to do little for her and insisted on staying put, and I complied. I slept in the room next to hers so I could listen for her at night.

When her condition hadn't improved after several days of bed rest, when she was having difficulty keeping down food and water, a friend finally talked us into going to the hospital. Just to get hydrated, we told Mother, and she finally relented, just for one IV. But the emergency crew panicked when they assessed her condition, ripping her gown open to slap on monitors and stick in tubes. Days later, when the breathing tube came out, and Mother was able to talk and eat again, she moaned, "If only we'd waited one more day at home."

Hardly anyone on earth was as willing to die as she was. She didn't harbor a morbid, depressive, suicidal death wish. There was just this quiet sense that she'd lived a full life and did not fear what came next. Deeply spiritual, she looked forward to spending eternity with Jesus, especially after so many years of compromised health. So many times she'd come to the edge of death and been rescued. How many more times could she stand to be rescued? Finally, the hospital released her and she returned home.

Me, I was still only thirty-eight years old—far too young, in my opinion, to lose my mother. We were just getting to be friends. We had just begun incorporating Mother into the new version of our family life. On occasion, she cooked dinner for us all. Malachi and my daughters, Meiko and Katja, hurried downstairs after school to hang out and play on her computer, and on weekends we'd huddle on her couch and watch movies. We felt enriched by Mother's presence in our lives.

But we live fast, we women of the Min family. We get right to task, don't waste time. Mother had graduated at the top of her high school class, gone right on to get her bachelor's degree in history, married my father immediately after graduation, and promptly had three kids. I swore I'd never choose such an oppressive life, forsaking a career for a husband and children. Wouldn't you know, though, I rushed through Barnard College in the mid-eighties, got married at the age of twenty-one, and produced three babies right away. This after cutting my teeth on feminism as a college student in the heady post–*Ms.* magazine/dawn of Generation X era! But we had been crazy in love, my young husband and I, and so together we chose this way of life and not only survived it, but made the most of it. Now I'm forty; my oldest is considering attending my alma mater, that bastion of feminist awakening; and I'm looking forward to enjoying my middle age as an empty-nester. I haven't forsaken a career, but I've definitely taken a roundabout path, writing and teaching.

Even though she never had a full-blown career, Mother led a full life, I realize now. She eventually obtained a graduate degree and engaged in a couple of part-time vocations. Especially, though, she devoted herself to volunteer work at her church and in ministry. She served as a spiritual leader in her community, a respected elder. So although she was relatively young in years when she came to live with us, only sixty-five, she'd accomplished much and felt ready to move on. Years of illness and spiritual practice had left her ready for death; she had overcome what yogis call *abhinivesa*: fear of death. She'd been practicing the "today is a good day to die" meditation for years.

In fact, none of us ever anticipated that she would have lived even this long. I'd known since I was fourteen that Mother had myasthenia gravis, so my brothers and I had grown up prepared to lose her early. No adult ever told us kids that her life span was likely to be shortened, but my eldest brother once informed me, his face wearing a knowing expression, that MG sufferers usually only lived fifteen to twenty years after diagnosis. How he figured this as a teenager, I don't know, but I believed him. It made sense, because of her frequent doctor's visits and multiple hospitalizations, her bouts of exhaustion on the couch.

Granted, Koreans appreciate death more than most. You hear "Ai-go chug-geh-da!"—oh God, I'm dying!—far more often than "Have a nice day." We've been called the Irish of Asia, and like the Irish, we are passionate and melodramatic. Koreans view death as honorable and meaningful. We feel friendly toward death, and we even bear a streak of martyrdom. No wonder Christianity spread so quickly and widely through South Korea: Jesus must've been Korean. He knew how to face death and make it matter, make it count. Mother, too, had lived in the presence of death for years, and now, having come so close, felt ready to shed earthly burdens.

A week after her release from the hospital, Mother collapsed again and went back to the Intensive Care Unit to be reconnected to IVs and monitors. The doctors urged us to consider the possibility of heart surgery, as at least one heart valve was not fully functional. As abhorrent as the notion of major surgery seemed, Mother figured she could do worse than dying on the table during a difficult operation. But when I mentioned her equanimity to the stylish, pony-tailed, fifty-something heart surgeon who had been highly recommended for his expertise with this particular procedure, he was insulted. "My patients don't die," he snapped.

And why not? I immediately disliked this surgeon. I hated his arrogance, the sports car I just knew he drove, the younger second wife I just knew he had. He wouldn't look me in the eye. He wouldn't sit down as he talked to us. Yet this was the man we might choose to perform the procedure that could save Mother's life—to plunge into her opened chest to sew one heart valve tighter, cut off the other two valves, and replace them with valves from pig's hearts. Only someone who believes he is God, I thought, could perform that outrageously invasive feat.

By now, though, I had grown accustomed to the arrogance of doctors. The less time they spent with you, the more important they were. Although visiting hours in the ICU began at eleven o'clock in the morning, I made a point of getting to the hospital early, seven or seven-thirty, so I could catch the doctors on their morning rounds. I never asked if I could come; I just walked in like I owned the place. Of course, my questions annoyed them. I probed them for information, queried them about their choices, the side effects of procedures and medications, and asked about alternatives. I listened and watched. I learned their lingo—"fibrillation," "cardiac output," "bi-pap"—and used it on them.

Although I've always wanted to appear mature and sophisticated, I'm stuck with a youthful appearance and manner. People regularly mistake me for a college student, and accordingly treat me like a kid. But in the ICU, speaking the language of the physicians, my status wasn't so clear. "Are you a doctor?" they'd ask me, one by one. Are you part of our club? How seriously should I take you? How much respect should I accord you? When they heard the truth, they'd turn to my mother and comment patronizingly, "What a good job you've done—such a bright daughter!" But the ICU nurses had started to discourage my early-morning visits because, they said, the doctors didn't have time to talk to me. "You're the only one who insists on coming early," they scolded. "Everyone else follows visiting hours."

Ah, the sexist hierarchy of the institution. Even in 2001, most of the doctors were male, while virtually the entire staff was female. I watched the nurses and therapists capitulate to the doctors who bustled in and out, dispensing plenty of orders but barely touching a patient. What could I do? Mother needed an advocate in the hospital with her. So I ignored the nurses' warnings and kept coming early. But at Mother's urging, I decided to be more diplomatic and less demanding. Sometimes I would sweet-talk the staff with baskets of snack foods from the gourmet grocer: imported cheese breadsticks, elegant Belgian cookies, organic berries. Nothing like food to smooth relations.

But what could we do for Mother? My brother had flown in from Oregon to meet with me and the doctors. What it came down to was this: take her home to let her slowly die, or choose the long shot of recovery through major cardiac surgery. We handed Mother over to the pony-tailed surgeon. The operation lasted seven hours. Just as planned, the surgeon broke Mother's sternum open, suspended her in a semi-alive state, actually stopping the heart from beating, and put the body on ice.

Thank God for e-mail. I'd been keeping friends abreast of Mother's condition by sending out a group message a couple of times a week. So when I asked for support on the day of the operation, friends from all over the city and neighboring areas dropped in to sit with us in the waiting room for a few minutes or a few hours. We filled the otherwise bleak space, rearranged the chairs, turned off the TV. As the valve job proceeded, the anesthesiologist phoned us every couple of hours with an update. In between his calls, my brother, friends, and I shared prayers, songs, silence, laughter, and take-out.

When it became clear that Mother would not recover from the neat work the cardiac surgeon had performed, we knew it was time to say goodbye, although she could have lived some weeks or months longer on life support. She was absolutely emphatic about not being suspended in an intubated brine. We had been saying goodbye for years already. What was one more goodbye?

In Korea, unlike in America, the aged are honored, treated with high respect just for being old. In Korea, you die in your eighties or nineties, of some normal condition like "old age"—without monitors and complicated diagnoses, without invasive treatments. Just the previous year, my maternal grandmother had passed away, at the age of eighty-five. Like many Korean elders, she died at home, surrounded by several generations of loved ones. Koreans still know how to die.

We talked about taking Mother home to die quietly, but it was too late. She wouldn't have survived the short car ride home. Despite all the meds and tubes, though, she remained conscious through the weeks of her final illness. On her last night, we all crowded into her ICU room—family, out-of-town relatives, friends, her pastor. One by one we said goodnight and embraced her a final time.

My brother and I took turns napping as she was weaned from life support. The morphine drip was slowly cranked up, and she fell unconscious late that night. At dawn, the morning nurse disconnected the last strand of support: the respirator. We listened to her harsh breathing slow down, then finally stop. We helped the nurse free her body from the tubes and needles that bound her. We continued to sit with her, stroking her still-warm body. What a relief to see that body liberated from its ravages and to feel her spirit set free. Finally, we let her be covered, closed the curtains, and walked out.

It was the twentieth of July, my daughter Katja's thirteenth birthday. When I was in labor with Katja, I had telephoned Mother in New York; we had planned that she would attend the birth and stay to help me out for a couple of weeks afterward. "Lie down! Don't give birth yet! I have to change my flight," she barked on the phone. Too late. Katja was born in the middle of the night, and Mother didn't arrive until the next day to cradle her newest grandchild. My older daughter, Meiko, almost two years old at the time, clearly felt possessive of her sister. "No! Mama's baby!" Meiko would shriek when she saw Mother holding Katja. So Mother would have to take Katja in her arms and hide behind a kitchen counter, on the floor, staring at the sleeping baby and smoothing her black hair.

Now I walked out of the hospital into the morning light, feeling like I'd given birth again. The summer air felt comfortably sticky and warm compared to the many hours of cool, dry hospital air. It was time to tend to the living. I went home, kissed my birthday girl, and sat down for strawberry crepes, her favorite breakfast. My husband stayed home from work. We lit a candle for Mother; it sat on the breakfast table as we feasted on ripe berries and cream. We'd finished crying. We just ate and talked and celebrated.

July, 2002

One morning, nearing the first anniversary of Mother's death—an important event in Korean tradition—I awoke with the image of a labyrinth in my mind. For Father's memorial, we'd held a special church service with family and friends, but I wanted to do something more personal for Mother. I'd been trying to think of a way to memorialize Mother, and now, thanks to this image, I knew how to proceed. That day I went to the library and began my research.

On Mother's memorial day, Katja's fourteenth birthday, I arose before sunrise and walked down the steep hill to the beach of Lake Michigan, just a few blocks from my house. I'd invited several friends, but it was still too early for them to arrive. I chose what seemed to me to be the perfect spot: close enough to the water for the sand to be firm, yet far enough from the main entrance to the beach to be relatively undisturbed. The air smelled dank, of dead alewives and rotting seaweed. The water was too cold to swim.

Clearing a spot in the sand, I picked up a stick and started to draw a labyrinth. It took several tries to get the right proportions and shape. Methodically I drew a three-circuit labyrinth about fifteen feet in diameter, a design I'd found in a book and had practiced drawing many times on paper. I lined the labyrinth's borders with rocks and shells and stuck a crow feather in the center. By now friends were starting to arrive. We gathered and, in silence, began walking through the labyrinth together, winding into the center of the circle, then brushing past each other on the way out. We walked slowly and in single file, walking mindfully with each step, creating imprints in the sand as we followed the spiraling curves of the labyrinth. Then, with the sun burning through the morning clouds, we sang "Amazing Grace" and "Be Like a Bird":

> Be like a bird, who halting in her flight
> On a limb too slight feels it give way beneath her,
> Yet sings, sings, knowing she has wings
> Yet sings, sings, knowing she has wings.

In the morning light we left Lake Michigan to walk up the steps. From the very top of the steps at the beach I looked down on our labyrinth. It looked like an alien formation, like a crop design. I left it as a visual prayer for Mother and walked home to my family. Katja would be waking up soon, and it was time to slice the strawberries.

Train Sounds

Ariel Gore

I lived in at least a dozen different places before I was six. The little wooden house in Pacific Grove where I was born. Bed and breakfast hotels in England. A leaky boat on an Amsterdam canal, a stone house in the French countryside. Places I cannot remember and there are no photographs of. The heartbeat percussion of a train in motion is as good as any lullaby. We were a family of four, then a family of three, chasing sanity through the early seventies.

We left my bio-dad along the way and moved into my grandmother's bright guest room back in California, then a tiny apartment behind a family famous only for their domestic disputes, then a commune overrun with naked children, and, finally, a converted garage in a suburban college town, a block away from the Catholic church where I caught my first glimpse of the priest who would soon become my new father.

We'd never been Catholics before, but now we went to morning and afternoon Mass. We washed our wandering sins away in the silver bowl of water at the entrance to the chapel. We took and ate the body of Christ, took and drank the bittersweet blood of Our Savior.

The priest looked ancient to me, gray hair thinning behind his ears, deep laugh lines around his mouth and eyes. He was bald on top, except for a wispy tuft of hair that stuck straight up in the middle. In my preschool illustrations of "The Last Supper," I drew Our

Savior as the priest: on his smiling pumpkin head, that wispy tuft of hair became a green-brown vine.

We moved in before the wedding—the priest, my mom, my older sister and me. Into the house on Lincoln Avenue surrounded by a cherry hedge in the college town south of San Francisco. I walked up and down the long wood-floor hall, counting each lap as a mile. Our new home was vast. Three whole bedrooms. A home office. A bathroom with tub *and* shower. Thick stucco walls. Terra-cotta-tiled roof. High, arched ceilings. Old mahogany doorframes. A makeshift chandelier made of Dixie cups. An antique clock never quite on time. The house my new father's father had built. 1920. My new father's childhood pets buried in the side garden. I studied their tombstones: Tippy the dog, Addison the squirrel.

Never mind the "step-" before the word "father," I understood that this was my ancestral home. My sister and I would sleep in the room our new father had shared with his brother; he and my mom would take over his parents' master bedroom. My mother and sister felt awkward at first, I learned later—as if they were stepping into someone else's garden—but I sprouted quick roots.

I turned six. My new father helped build the wooden play structure at the elementary school he'd attended some fifty years before. "My dad built it," I bragged to my new schoolmates.

I turned eight. My new father told me stories from the Depression. About the nights he'd lay awake listening to his parents argue about money. About his little-boy terror. *Would they lose the house?*

Those olden days seemed unfathomably unstable. I planted sage in the backyard, listened to my owl in the oak tree outside my bedroom window. The *hoot hoot* lulled me to sleep like a train's horn.

I turned ten. We traveled to the Sierras every summer just like my father had done as a boy.

I turned twelve, uncovered decades-old mosaics buried on the garden floor.

Lucky were we. No Depression. And even though my mother was an artist who rarely worked for money and my now-excommunicated priest of a father only earned five dollars an hour at the bookstore, the house was paid off. The bank didn't own it. We did. Bury anything you like in this earth. It's ours. It will always be here. My hamster, Cinnamon, was laid to rest in a grave next to Tippy's.

I turned sixteen, and my feet started to itch. I dropped out of high school and ran away. I lived in dozens of places as I chased freedom through the late eighties. A grimy hostel in Hong Kong, a dorm room in Beijing. A hammock on the South China Sea, squats in Amsterdam and London, a little stone house in the Italian countryside where, at age nineteen, I gave birth to a baby girl, rocked her to sleep by train sounds. But even at my most angst-ridden and angry, I knew I always had a home to return to.

Permanence is such a sham.

I turned thirty-three, and it happened. The unimaginable. We lost the house. A second mortgage taken out in the roaring nineties, "conservatively" invested and quickly lost when George W. hijacked the economy, meant tenants. A reappraisal meant taxes. My parents moved to Mexico and my new father, now eighty-five, announced that he would never return. "I'm too old to travel," he explained. Things led to things and pretty soon it was gone, the bones of childhood pets and all.

I hadn't lived in the house on Lincoln Avenue in years, didn't want to. The town that had grown up around my ancestral home was part of Silicon Valley now: yuppie-greed unbearable. Still. I wept for seven days and seven nights. We. Lost. The. House.

"Imagine how you'd feel if you were a Haitian refugee," my mother offered over the phone.

And I said, "Yeah, that's part of my grief. Knowing I'm such a wimp-ass."

When the sale finalized, my father's heart stopped—but only for a minute. It wasn't time to join the ancestors just yet.

"I'm sorry all this is happening," I told him when I called his hospital room at *la clinica*, but he just laughed. "I'm not angry about it," he said. "These things happen when you're old."

I guess I'm not so Zen. Night after night I dreamed of the ghosts I had come to know so well. The earthy opera singer grandmother.

The professor great-grandfather who watched us from his sepia-tinted portrait over the dining room table. Tippy the dog in his bronze-plaqued grave. The spinster Aunt Minna, wiry and stern in the old photographs, for whom we set a place at the table every night. "Minna's here," my new father would say before we started eating—our invisible dinner guest.

I longed for all of it: my thick stucco walls, my owl, my uncovered mosaics, the ease with which I could make myself at home as a child. And I cursed the new owner's fortune. Even my daughter, now fourteen, cried. The house she was brought to as an infant when we had nowhere else to go. The home where she was baptized by the pumpkin-head priest she called "Nonno."

I grieved this home more intensely than I have ever grieved a human's passing. Humans are supposed to die. Ashes scattered in gardens on ancestral land. Replaced by newborns. But the earth? The home? I was not prepared. We. Lost. The. House.

I wake up in a panic. I want to drive down to the Bay Area from my Northwestern rental, sneak into the new owners' yard, and uproot my sage plants. *These are mine.* But where would I replant them?

Sorrow and outrage push me into a weird, disciplined, manic mode I have never known before. At the corner coffee shop, I meet with a dreadlocked real estate agent. "I have no money, am self-employed, and have really bad credit. What can you do for me?" She sets down her café latte and hands me a list of instructions that I think might be designed to make me face reality and *forget it.*

But I'm not interested in reality. I start calling old creditors and pleading my case. I even restructure my business. *Build me a miracle,* I implore the ancestors, *like only you can.* I have never owned anything before, never wanted to. I've valued my portability above all. But now I can think of nothing but the fact that I need somewhere to plant my sage.

The mortgage broker gives me a budget: $160,000 in a town where anything under $200,000 sells in an hour. The real estate agent sends me listings for neglected asbestos deathtraps and brand-new particleboard constructions on the outskirts of town. I drive fast, but the developers always get there first. My daughter looks like she'll cry as we tour "our price range." Unbalanced structures that smell of mildew.

"We could move to Ohio," I offer. Tears well up in her eyes.

One morning, we drive out to a ramshackle hut whose owner has died. The key in the lock box won't even open the door. "What do you *want*?" I whisper to the ancestors as, once again, we start to walk away dejected. And suddenly, at that very moment, a new "For Sale by Owner" sign appears in my field of vision. It hadn't been there the day before.

"This will do," I think I hear someone whisper. I point, smiling.

The real estate agent dials the number on the flyer, then hands me the phone because the voice on the other end doesn't want to talk to agents.

"You want to see my home?" It's a man's voice, low and warm.

Yes. I do.

A tiny wooden house on a tiny unlandscaped lot, built in the rail yard in 1912. Hush. I can hear the train coming now.

"The house has been well loved," the voice assures me. "It has a good history."

Other sellers boast of square footage and new vinyl siding, but this one knows what's important. We meet the following morning. Refinished hardwood floors. Almost two bedrooms. A clawfoot tub in the bathroom. A little dining nook where Aunt Minna could pull up her chair.

"Do the passing trains keep you up at night?" I want to know.

He smiles, shakes his head. "You don't like train sounds?"

"No. I like 'em fine."

4.

Problem?
What Problem?

If the shoe doesn't fit, must we change the foot?

—Gloria Steinem

The Flight

Joyce Thompson

We sit at the kitchen table, playing War. We've been playing the same game for more than an hour, the piles of
cards before us shrinking and growing as our fortunes ebb and flow.
My daughter is six years old and wholly engrossed in the game.
Numbers and their order are a lesson worth learning. Besides, both
the baby and her father are napping, and she has me all to herself,
something which is all too rare.

It is gray outside the kitchen window, and the river mouth is
swollen from an unseasonably rainy autumn, so that the estuary
islands have disappeared earlier than usual, drowned till spring.
Clouds fluffy and glum as the pelt of a gray fox rub against the far
landmass, obscuring the dunes. The gentle predictability of the game
is soothing. Inside me certainty grows. This is the day. I can hardly
believe it, yet it is even harder to believe that I'll back down. The rest
of my life is a huge wave pressing against a fragile dike. I realize I've
been waiting for the end of the game, but the game goes on and on,
too straightforward and simpleminded for me to lose on purpose. As
soon as the baby wakes up, I tell myself. Then.

"Mommy, play," my daughter demands.

I play. My six takes her two. Her nine wins over my four. At last,
I hear the baby whimper, waking. "Put on your shoes and coat," I tell
my daughter. "I'm going to change your brother. Then we'll go to the

147

store."

"Can't we finish the game first?" she asks.

"You're too good for me," I say. "I'll never beat you. I give up."

"Don't give up, Mommy."

"We have to get to the store before it closes. I have to buy some things for dinner." I reach across the table and squeeze her little hand. "Shoes. Coat. Now."

"Can I get a treat at the store?" she asks. I tell her we'll see.

I take a moment to pet the dog on our way to the car. By the time I start the engine, my heart's turned from a bee into a wrecking ball, slamming so hard against my chest wall I can't imagine the neighbors won't come to their windows to see what's wrong, that my husband won't wake up from his nap. Soon enough, we are out of the driveway. Soon enough, we are driving past the store.

"Mommy! Aren't you going to stop?"

I take a deep breath. "You know what? Since it's a holiday, I thought we'd take a little drive. We can go to the store in Seaside for a change."

"I was born in Seaside," my daughter says. "It's a long way away."

"Not so far without traffic. We'll be there before you know it."

The old soul we call the baby has been vested for a bit more than one year in this lifetime. In the rearview mirror I can see him in his car seat behind me, staring contemplatively out the window at the monochrome afternoon. As soon as it's topographically possible to catch a signal, I put the radio on and turn up the volume, hoping sheer noise will keep my daughter from monitoring our course, but even though her reading is still iffy, she knows the terrain. "Mommy! This is where you get off for Seaside," she cries out, as we speed by the exit.

"They have a special on pork chops in Astoria, " I tell her. "You know how much you like pork chops."

I am always watching behind me, expecting to see the roving red light of the state patrol. I expect to be arrested, to be taken back. Nothing appears in the mirror except the occasional delivery truck, the errant gas-guzzling passenger car, the camper trailer on its way home from California. Adrenaline breaks in waves inside me, sickening and exhilarating at the same time. The farther away we get, the less likely it seems that I will turn the car around and go back. I drive deep into old Astoria until I find an ATM. I tell my daughter I need to get money for the pork chops.

Twilight is gray on gray, sucking the last traces of color out of the day. The mist turns to drizzle, still a little too intermittent to keep the wipers on and a Sunday evening call-in show replaces country-western laments on the radio. I surf the dial until I pick up the community college station, playing rock and roll. My daughter turns restless, thrashing inside her seatbelt. Last chance. Last chance, I tell myself. My nerves are fixed at a permanent high vibration, above the range of human hearing. I hope my circuit breakers are working. Otherwise I may explode.

"Mommy! Why are we getting on the bridge? Isn't this the way to Grandma and Grandpa's house?"

"You're right," I tell her. "I was going to make it a surprise, but you're much too sharp for me to fool. Won't it be fun to visit Grandma and Grandpa?"

"Why isn't Daddy coming?"

Can I say it out loud? If I say it, it will be true. Mommy is leaving Daddy. We are running away from home.

It was a hard summer. It's been a hard fall. It's been a hard eleven years, with just enough sweetness to make me believe my life must not be unbearable.

I have not been entirely alone since early September, when I defied his wishes and drove my stepdaughter, his natural child, to college for the first time. He was ready to let her find her own damn way there, this for the sin of inviting a high school friend to join the family for a last picnic on the beach. He followed us up the driveway, yelling. I drove away. Because my children were there, I came back. Almost as if he sensed my intention, he has not left the house for more than a few minutes, scarcely left my side for almost three months. I imagine people who live at the foot of a volcano fall under a spell like this one. The eruptions are widely spaced enough in time that even though the mountain is always rumbling, even though you are always afraid, you somehow convince yourself it is not essential to move, not quite yet. Just when you least expect it, the volcano blows. Except really, you always expect it. Life is flinch. Hope is somebody else's pet.

But this is it. I would rather walk on hot coals than tread the brittle edges of his anger anymore. Who knows how I have chosen this day? Who knows where I've found the courage? Who knows what will become of us?

It's dark now, raining for real. I turn the fan on full so heat will reach the baby in the backseat. My daughter stares at me, still waiting for an answer.

"Mommy's leaving Daddy," I say. It's no secret to this child that our house is not a safe and happy place. I suppose I halfway expect her to be grateful. On the other hand, and I understand this too late, our house is the only home she knows. She starts to cry. Following her lead, sensing her sorrow, the baby too starts crying.

And so, at last, do I.

Smells Like Perfume Inserts

Ayun Halliday

Either your cancer goes into remission or you die. You dump the abusive gorilla you wish you'd never met or you remain with him to the end, cringing, wondering if one of these days he'll smack you hard enough to kill you. You perish from exposure, or you use your pocketknife to sever the foot that's stuck in the crevice, fashion a tourniquet from your favorite T-shirt and crawl down the mountain in subzero temperatures, nourishing yourself on snow and a small bag of airline peanuts. If you survive, get yourself an agent and prepare to weep as Mare Winningham or Meredith Baxter Birney plays you in the made-for-TV movie about your courage in the face of adversity.

Not all of us get to have some huge, barely surmountable obstacle to surmount, though we do all get to die sooner or later. (Dang.) I'm not saying that getting attacked by an alligator or disfigured by burning jet fuel would make me feel important; it's just dismaying that my myriad problems are small and mainstream, so generic that they could belong to anybody. It galls me that my obstacles help sell shitty magazines intended for American women other than myself. Big weirdoes aren't a part of their demographic, probably because we're so resistant to makeovers. Of course, little weirdoes are, so once upon a time, I pored over every diet, wardrobe, relationship, and lifestyle tip I could get my hands on, figuring that by the time I turned eighteen, I'd know everything I would need to make a fresh, perfect start. In hindsight, Flannery O'Connor, Janis Joplin, and my high school art teacher were far more influential in determining the way I would turn out. Whoo, that was a close one.

Do magazines that cater exclusively to women's so-called interests exert similar influence in Afghanistan or Sierra Leone? *Fifteen Fresh Ideas for Avoiding Stoning? Treat Your Stump to Spring's Hottest Looks? Turn That Unexploded Mine into a Festive Holiday Centerpiece and 98 Other Super Simple Crafts Your Kids Will Love!*

Sagging stomachs, overstuffed closets, failure to snack sensibly, unbecoming hairdos, inability to dress appropriately for business interviews, inadequate protection from the sun's burning rays, poorly applied cosmetics, dumpy-looking living rooms, defiant toddlers, husbands we've forgotten how to stimulate, dinner parties that fizzle, malevolent coworkers passively endured, odors both real and imaginary—shouldn't these be celebrated for what they are? Here's one way of looking at it: anyone who dreads bathing-suit season hasn't spent time under a burkah. To put it another way, if some editorially brain-dead piece of shiny can make me feel bad about my aging skin, I must not be facing chemotherapy! Comparatively speaking, I don't have a care in the world—in which case, *those fucking magazines* can be my big problem.

So can their celebrity cover girls, at least until such time as *I* become famous and buff or the worst thing I can imagine happening to me happens to me, or worse, my children. I'm wondering when, if ever, one of those gorgeous, privileged cover-creatures will use the platform she's been given for social good, rather than complaining about the paparazzi, the press, and how she wishes everyone would stop bringing up her old boyfriend. Newsflash: most of the rest of us would love it if someone else would bring up our exes, because we're getting pretty sick of always having to do it ourselves, as are our husbands. If they're not going to give us some uncensored, white-hot Hollywood gossip, perhaps these role models could address vital issues, like how maybe we should stop shopping at the big national discount store that pays its overworked employees slave wages while funneling millions of dollars into organizations bent on destroying subsidized health- and childcare. I'm not saying that the stars have to start shopping there in order to stop shopping there. They can continue paying their personal assistants' six-figure salaries to pick up cat food on Rodeo Drive, content that they've inspired a few of us lumpy, low-budget, uncelebrated types to suck it up and spend forty cents more for Meow Mix from someplace less Satanic. If they insist on dwelling on their personal lives, the text should go something like: "Your readers are right to envy me! My god, I'm pushing forty, but I've got the body of a twenty-year-old modern dancer. Thankfully, I've got more money than I could spend in five lifetimes, because my personal trainers, personal chefs, and the personal gyms I've had installed in my four homes don't come cheap! Why, the Italian marble in my bathroom alone costs more than sending every child in Chicago's Cabrini Green housing project to Harvard Law School! Plus, I never have to clean my own toilet, I fucked George Clooney and I get to wear sequins, like, every weekend! It's crazy! I'm so lucky!" Wouldn't that be refreshing?

With the magazines' celebrity profiles made over to my satisfaction, I'd like to propose a radical overhaul of their boilerplate stories. Pandering to womanly paranoia is obviously working, from a business standpoint. The publishers would balk at screwing with that profitable template, but what about the content? This easy test will prove just how stale it's become. Ready? Okay, quick, give me a way to combat holiday depression. You said, "Choose healthy, low-fat snacks from the buffet table over empty calories that'll make you feel bad about yourself later," didn't you? Of course you did, because that's the same glossy advice they've been printing in their December issues since before I could read! Perhaps in rural Zambia, it might be news that a woman can save herself from the "holiday blues" by nibbling on celery (no French Onion Dip! no French Onion Dip!), but for those whose culture has been thoroughly permeated, how about some less predictable copy? Like: "Snatch a handful of bourbon balls and lock yourself in the bathroom, whispering 'I hate you! I hate you! I hate you!' until the urge to physically attack your most obstreperous in-law subsides somewhat."

Also, it would be nice if all their recipes and craft instructions were accompanied by photographs depicting some pathetic piece of garbage that looks even lamer than the average American woman's first attempt at making the featured item will. This will be a relief to anyone who's ever spent five tearful hours hot-gluing seashells onto a cheap picture frame. Take away the professional stylists, lighting designers, and photographers and show that super summer project for what it really is—a colossal waste of time, unless of course you're five years old and seashell-covered picture frames are the kindergartners' special Valentine for their mommies, in which case I'll treasure it forever.

Finally, if one of those rags ever snaps me unawares, galumphing up Broadway, bra straps showing, hair pulled into pigtails more flaccid than flirty, in pants that make my big abdomen look even bigger, I dare them to try to place a black bar over my eyes. I'm not ashamed that their don'ts are my dos. I'm lumpy, blotchy, occasionally intemperate, saggy, baggy, big, weird, and comparatively speaking, problem-free, knock on wood. My loved ones and I are healthy; we have a poorly decorated but uncondemned apartment and a lot of high-fat foods in our dirty refrigerator—and we're not even on the Atkins Diet! (Can we get a celebrity feature on how the torture chambers of factory farms will remain a big fat mother-trucking problem until we put the brakes on meat consumption?) I'm fortunate to live in a country that allows me to wear what I want, read what I want, sleep with whom I want—in theory, anyway—and point out its many imperfections, even if I have no pat solutions for cleaning up her unsightly blemishes.

Stepping Off the Mommy Track

Laura Fraser

In the back of my closet, there's a box with a set of maternity clothes inside. They're my size—or would be if I were pregnant. Each time I sift through my stuff to give away things I no longer wear, I pause and hold that box in my hand, considering. It was a little premature, I admit, to buy maternity clothes before the stick had turned blue. But five years ago, when I saw that big-bellied black mini-dress and tunic top, I was so sure I was soon to become one of those hip moms-to-be that I bought them anyway.

The box sat in the back of the closet while my husband and I made up baby names and debated whether we could afford to move to a neighborhood with better schools. It was still there on the day I decided to go off the Pill, which was, not coincidentally, the day my husband suggested that perhaps we should wait, that he wasn't quite sure he was ready to have a baby.

And then, just a few weeks later, the box got more room in the closet when my husband moved his clothes out. Not only had he realized that he didn't want to have a baby, but he didn't want to be with me, period. I was thirty-six, and heartbroken. Still, I wasn't worried about not having a family. I figured it wouldn't be long before I found a new husband—a dad for the children I took for granted I would someday have.

But it wasn't so easy to find that new guy. Being single with forty on the near horizon was quite different from flitting about on the wide plains of thirty. A lot of men seemed nervous that a woman my age might be more interested in finding a father for her unborn child than in finding a partner for herself. They seemed to have a sixth sense that a woman my age might be, well, a woman like me.

Thirty-six passed, and thirty-seven, tick tock, and thirty-eight.

Obviously, I've never made having children the highest priority in my life. Like many women my age, I've always paid more attention to my work, my sweetie, and my travel plans than to when I was going to have kids. I pressed the snooze button on my biological clock, assuming I'd just wake up one day with children bouncing on the bed.

But when I didn't land another mommy-track relationship right away, I had to confront the question of having a child on my own. Why not reverse the order of my plans: first have the child and then find the man? Men, after all, age better than eggs.

For months I imagined having a baby, somehow, on my own. I'd wrap her up like a papoose and take her to my office, where she would sleep quietly while I worked. I'd bundle him in his stroller and he'd nap while I went to the gym. I'd come home, fix myself a nice dinner with a glass of wine, curl up with a long novel, and she'd be right there, snoozing along. The only problem was that in my fantasies of being a single mom, the kid slept all the time. Not a good sign.

There are people who can handle being single parents. I admire them. I just have a feeling I wouldn't be one of them. Aside from my somewhat precarious financial situation, I have an independent streak a mile wide. I've managed my career with the goal of being my own boss. Having a child might teach me patience, but I'm no saint. I'd need someone to hand the child off to once in a while. And I would have to give up many of the things I cherish—traveling, making spontaneous plans, spending time alone. I'd be willing to make those sacrifices, but not without some company. Not by myself.

Ultimately, I knew myself well enough to know that being a single mother simply wouldn't be a wise move. But I wasn't having any luck on the finding-a-dad front, either. Babies just don't seem to be in the cards for me, not in this lifetime.

I feel fine about my decision until I catch a toddler's smile while standing in line at the post office. I yearn to smell that hair, to touch those tiny toes, to feel that in a world of so many disappointed affections, someone loves me unconditionally, at least until that someone turns thirteen. I think of how wonderful my relationship with my parents is these days and that I'll never have a daughter my age when I'm seventy, never have grandchildren. In those moments, the loss is overwhelming.

But letting go of the idea of having children has also brought me a sense of clarity. I want to find a partner who fits into the rhythms of my heart, not one who merely shares my interest in procreation. In the meantime, I have several nephews, a niece, and a small boy next door who adores me, and vice versa. I'm the crazy aunt who wouldn't have half as much time to bang on drums, send postcards from exotic places, and write Christmas stories if she had children of her own.

I've just turned forty, and while I know that I probably have a few years left to have a child, the chances aren't good. I've come to accept that, and I've gotten on with my life. Still, I'm not throwing away that box in the back of my closet. Not quite yet.

Just Say I Do

Merrill Markoe

I've been giving a lot of thought to the idea of getting married lately. Ever since President Bush decided to go out on a limb and give "marriage" his ringing endorsement, thereby proposing another forward-thinking political initiative on behalf of the Republican party that may at long last lay the groundwork for a full slate of all the other things your mother always told you to do, such as getting the hair out of your eyes, standing up straight, changing your tone of voice when you talk to me, and not leaving the house looking like that.

The conservative Republican agenda, of course, is to address the considerable pressure being applied by right-wing religious organizations to back a Constitutional amendment banning same-sex marriage. This, despite the fact that everyone knows that it is heterosexual couples who are responsible for the current 50 percent divorce rate. And of the other 50 percent, the ones who do sustain long-term marriages, it is wise not to make too many sweeping generalizations. I still remember a story I read in the *LA Times* about a woman who set fire to her husband of thirty-five years because he ate her chocolate Easter bunny, thus proving that longevity in marriage is not always a good way to evaluate its success.

Opponents of same-sex marriage like to cite the ability to have children as the significant line of demarcation between a real marriage and a fraudulent facsimile. However, in making this case, it seems like they conveniently forget to mention some of the famous offspring alumni of "real marriage." For example, Adolf Hitler, the Enron guys, the terrorists who engineered 9/11, and every serial killer of the twentieth century.

Statistically speaking, in fact, gay marriage stands alone as the last outpost of marriage's most pristine ideals, since same-sex couples are the only ones whose marital track records are untarnished. If we are going to question the validity of these marriages, then that proposed Constitutional amendment ought to contain a sub-clause restricting certain heterosexual unions that have, in the fullness of time, proven to be totally futile. For instance, the marriages of movie stars to anyone, straight or gay, especially if they have participated in a *People* magazine article in which they have declared that they are "very much in love." Or weddings involving people under twenty-eight who have known each other for less than a year and are intending to say their vows while wearing a parachute, scuba gear, or anything else that celebrates their hobbies.

In fact, when you look at the big picture, it is easy to conclude that the best thing for our culture might be to just give marriage to the gay community and let them refurbish it the way they do run-down neighborhoods. Then, once they have restored it to its original authentic beauty, plus added all the modern upgrades, heterosexuals can be permitted to return and continue their pattern of systematic debasement.

But here's the part about the whole issue of who can get married and who cannot that *really* has me puzzled. Back in February 2004, when San Francisco Mayor Gavin Newsom started issuing marriage licenses to same-sex partners, three thousand gay couples rushed to the altar. That's *six thousand* adults who were so anxious for the opportunity to be eligible to sue each over common property, pay alimony, and take out mutual restraining orders, that they couldn't wait another minute. And that's what I found unsettling. Not because the idea of gay marriage gives me pause, but precisely because the only marriage I seem to have a real problem with is my own. As a cer-

tified straight person (and yes, I did take the trouble to become certi-
fied), I have been legally permitted to get married for over four
decades. Yet never once have I been able to motivate myself suffi-
ciently to push a relationship further in that direction. Although I
have been much lived-togethered, I have never been down an aisle
that doesn't have something I need on sale.

It isn't because I haven't had access to successful relationships. I
have been in a really good one now for the past three years, perhaps
my best one ever. In it, not only have I learned to talk through dis-
agreements instead of driving around for hours in my car with a
packed suitcase, but I have gazed with astonishment at my partner
while he actually listens to me talk. I even have proof; I have given
him a number of pop quizzes. And still I remain the quiet calm spot
in a tornado of peer group weddings, the only one who has never
made all her friends shell out money to buy her silver and crystal and
matching flatware, and therefore does not yet have any of the aforementioned and is frankly a little pissed off about the whole thing.
Especially when I add it all up, and realize that I have paid for so
many sets of other people's pricey wedding registry china that I could
easily host a dinner for the entire State Department, if I could stand
to be in their presence.

Oh sure, the first guy I lived with played the marriage card during our breakup in one of those desperate, eleventh-inning
maneuvers that I never fall for because they remind me of nothing so
much as an evening of avant-garde theater. And the next guy and I
actually once went and had premarital blood tests. But I think it was
because he just liked going to the doctor. In his perfect world, a marriage license would also have required a brain scan, an electrocardi-
ogram and a syphgmomanometer reading.

The key point here is that it wasn't as if I were the poor little
wan and weeping thing who was left at the altar, or the frail victim of
heartless commitment-phobic womanizers (although, of course, I
have enjoyed the company of such men on many delightful occasions). No, I had no intention of ever marrying any of the guys I have
loved. I've never even had a fantasy about how my wedding would

be. Occasionally I would want the men who claimed to love me to say that they would like to marry me, but it was more an exercise in positive reinforcement, like when you make someone tell you over and over that they don't think you look fat.

When my father was dying, I asked him what he considered the biggest success in his life. When, without hesitation, he answered, "My marriage," it made me wonder for a moment if he was a closet polygamist. Because the marriage I saw him in was one that sounded like this: "I SAID I love you. Now what the hell else do you WANT from me for Chrissakes?"

On a related topic, not long ago I was reading through my childhood diaries and I found that as early as fifth grade I wrote, "I am never getting married. I am never having kids." Of course, a couple of pages later I also wrote, "I am never having my period." Though apparently I had the foresight to rethink that one.

So why then, when I attended someone's wedding recently and the bride threw the bouquet to me, did I turn and duck so it bounced off my shoulder? Why does the idea of announcing to the world in a ceremony that you belong to someone and they to you forever and ever give me the feeling that I am tied to a chair in a windowless room, unable to reach the phone to find the number of Rush Limbaugh's doctor so that I can beg him to prescribe me some of that OxyContin? The craziest part of it all is that I like the idea of being in a relationship with someone I love. And when I'm in one, I do my best to make the object of my affections happy. I have even been known to take a Vivarin at midnight in order to cook and serve dinner at three in the morning, when my beloved sometimes shows up and is hungry.

Which is why I find myself wondering: what do those six thousand gay people in San Francisco have in their hearts that I don't have in mine, besides an obsession with Barbra Streisand? What do they—and all the much-married people of America—know about love that I have yet to comprehend?

But then, as soon as I find myself romanticizing, I begin to think: if other people have so much more emotional depth than I do, why are there so many marriages that last only a few months? Or marriages where the sex has been dead for decades? Why is there so much cheating and complaining, why so many vile postmarital lawsuits where both people are not only trying to rob each other of everything they own, but also imposing stiff penalties for having been stupid enough to agree to the marriage in the first place? Why are there women who marry one violence-prone alcoholic—or drug addict or pedophile—after another? What rational justification can there be for the marital track record of an Elizabeth Taylor or a Liza Minnelli? And then when I think about all that, I wind up right back where I started.

Which brings me to the only solution to my dilemma that I can think of. If I could get the President and his band of goofballs to pass a Constitutional amendment prohibiting *me* from getting married, I feel fairly certain that there would be nothing that could keep me from insisting on getting married as soon as possible. Suddenly, like all those marriage-hungry couples of the gay community, there would be nothing that I could imagine wanting more.

Naked Pictures

Sefi Atta

Good thing this happened the week before Lent. My nine-year-old daughter, Temi, and a group of her friends were pretending to be in an art competition during the after-hours program at their Catholic school here in Mississippi. One of the kids suggested, "Hey, why don't we all draw a picture of A Bad Marriage?" His drawing was half man, half animal. Temi's was a naked woman with two C's for breasts, standing next to a naked man with a U between his legs. The man had a bubble coming out of his mouth with the words, "Baby, wanna come to my bedroom?"

Temi thought the drawings were funny, and I imagine how she laughed, with her mouth wide open and her two lower incisors missing. I never asked who won their contest, but she and her friends must have gotten distracted, because they soon abandoned art for some other activity. That must have been when their after-hours supervisor found the pictures. She held them up and asked, "Who drew these?" Temi and her friend put their hands up. The after-hours supervisor marched them to the principal's office.

I heard about the naked pictures when I came to pick up Temi for her piano lesson. She was the tallest girl in the third grade, but the top of her head barely reached my armpits and she was trying to block me with her chest. "I'll tell you in the car," she said. "It's something. I'll tell you. Mom-ee."

I hugged her to reassure her, and noticed how the after-hours supervisor kept glancing at us. Then as I signed the register, the supervisor said the principal wanted to have a word with me.

I was ten years old in 1974, living in Nigeria. That was the year my mother sent me to Queen's College for girls, a boarding school about ten miles from our family's home in the city of Lagos. I was there for four years, until my mother transferred me to another boarding school, this one in England. At Queen's, if the principal wanted to see a pupil, it meant she was going to whip her with a switch and then make her kneel on the cement corridor outside. This principal—and I actually had great affection for her; her punishments were merely the norm in Nigeria—once beckoned to me when I was wearing flip-flops with my navy school pinafore, which was against the rules. "Come here," was all she said, and I wet myself.

Temi's principal in Mississippi was barely taller than Temi. She was slim, blond, and walked around grinning and swinging her arms. She never raised her voice. She and I were about the same age. I stepped into her office that afternoon, a forty-year-old woman in 2004. I wasn't the one in trouble, and I wanted to cry. Then Temi threw herself into my lap and sobbed as her principal showed me the drawing, and I had put aside my phobia of school offices to tell Temi how proud I was of her. She thought she would be suspended, the picture would go on her permanent record, and her life would be over.

I said to the principal, "I didn't raise her to be embarrassed about nakedness," which was, admittedly, rather self-righteous, and as I patted Temi's trembling belly, I was thinking, my daughter thinks a bad marriage is one in which a couple are having sex?

Temi stopped crying only when I confessed I'd drawn naked pictures myself as a child. I asked the principal if I could keep the drawing, and it crossed my mind to add that I wanted to hang it up on our refrigerator with the rest of our family photos, but I'd trained myself to resist such contrary tendencies.

"You may," the principal said with a smile. "I don't think I need it for evidence."

Temi and I had left her office and were buckled up in my car when I thought, *Evidence of what?*

I'd always been one of the more low-profile parents at that school. I'd volunteered for fests and supervised class parties and attended Mass on Thursdays, even though I didn't take communion—my mother was an Anglican, my late father was a Moslem, and I attended Koranic lessons and church. (In time, religion had become quite confusing for me.) But I wasn't Class Mom, didn't sit on any board. I wasn't one of the mothers who spent as much time in school as the teachers did—again, because of my "tendencies." I heard these moms, at PTA and other school meetings, making such statements as, "We love our kids. That's why we're all here today," and I avoided their calls for parental participation, because their definition of love wasn't the same as mine. Every morning, I dropped Temi off at the school entrance. Every morning, she said she didn't need me to walk her to class. Really, what she said was, "Why would you do that?" Also, she asked that I change out of the gray sweats I wore every morning, if I intended to escort her into the school. Yeah, she was proud of me, she said, but the sweats were kind of yucky.

People in her school knew I was a writer. About a year before the naked pictures, to promote the annual Accelerated Reading drive, the school newsletter ran an article about me and another writer mom. Temi was featured in the same newsletter because she was the first in the school to reach her yearly reading goal. Despite my preference to keep a low profile, I had agreed to be included, partly because I wanted my daughter to stop saying, "Move your lazy butt. Only Daddy works in this house." She was kidding, but she did think Daddy's work was more important than mine. He was a Nigerian-trained doctor on a government-sponsored program for underserved U.S. communities, which was the reason we were in Mississippi.

I also wanted Temi to have bragging rights, for a change. She thought she was a nerd because she enjoyed reading, and I hoped that certain mothers, who had deduced from my yucky sweats that I didn't have a job, might stop looking at me as if they expected me to get more involved in the school, or at least pay more attention to my appearance whenever I showed up.

The newsletter article included a quote about my gratitude to God for the gift of writing. I *was* thankful, but God already knew. I had imagined, however, that the pious postscript would be appropriate, because the other writer mom had privately revealed to me that she volunteered some of her time in service to the Lord. Unlike me, she wasn't a Pharisee, so she didn't need to flaunt her faith in the newsletter.

The librarian of the school kept asking to read my work, after that newsletter. This woman had such a gracious spirit, and I'd seen the way she welcomed children every morning. Sometimes we hugged. She thought I was humble for saying my stories were best kept at home. She had no clue that there were characters in my stories who cussed and challenged the Church for demonizing the Yoruba gods, Obatala, Shango, Yemoja and Oshun. The Yorubas believed that in the beginning, all the world was water. The gods came down on a chain carrying a calabash filled with soil, a cockerel, and a chameleon. They poured the soil over the water. The cockerel spread it around, the chameleon walked on it to make sure it was safe, and other gods followed. The Christian missionaries labeled the Yorubas who worshipped these gods as pagans: they had no holy books or hymns; they chanted to drumbeats and worshipped in shrines adorned with carvings of naked bodies, which, in their simplicity, reminded me of Temi's pictures.

I was trying to be as unobtrusive as I possibly could in her school, and there were, therefore, fights I avoided fighting. Once, a teacher's assistant in charge of the Accelerated Reading program refused to increase her reading level, because, she said, Temi already borrowed books from the school library that were beyond her level. All I said was, "That's fine. So long as she can continue to read the books she wants to read." Another time, an eleven-year-old boy in the after-hours program, tall enough to pass for thirteen, and good at sports—a jock, Temi explained—grabbed her by her collar in a rowdy football game. He yanked her to her feet, yelling, "Give me the ball or else." The after-hours supervisor gave him a time-out and told Temi to carry on playing "as if nothing had happened." This time, I called the principal to report the boy for bullying, and she saw that he apologized to Temi. I didn't complain about the insensitive way in which the supervisor had counseled Temi.

So there had been some problems, but I didn't expect my daughter to go through life without learning how to overcome trials. The school was still the best option for her. It was cozier than the public school; it was racially integrated, unlike the one private school in the city; and it was the most liberal of the Christian schools around.

Having made a deliberate choice to enroll Temi in the school, I believed it was necessary to show my respect by not criticizing the values of the staff and other parents. After all, imagine the reverse situation, in which an American would tell me, on the subject of Queen's College in Nigeria, "Sounds like the atmosphere there was pretty oppressive, and that's probably why you have an aversion to authority figures and passive-aggressive tendencies." I also knew that there were adults, school staff included, who could retaliate against a child. I had been seventeen, attending the English boarding school, when a teacher came within an inch of my ear with her coffee breath. Since I hadn't completed her vacation assignment, she said, I would fail my "A" level exams. My mother had written to the school headmaster to protest that no teacher had the right to predict my future. But I never reported what this teacher had done next because I was worried I might get her sacked. "Bitch," she had whispered in my ear.

When Temi and I got home, I sat down to type a letter to the principal about the naked pictures. I used words like "puritanical" and "censorship." I objected to the way she was treated, and asked what exactly the drawing was evidence of, besides her creative ability. I wasn't worried that the principal's reprimand would shape Temi's evolving idea of sexuality; I was just furious and sad that Temi was shamed. Ironically, when I asked if she approved of my letter, Temi said, "Yes, because I have protection."

The same week, two pre-kindergarten children began kissing on the floor during the after-hours program. The boy was on top of the girl. The after-hours supervisor, the same one who had noticed the naked pictures, separated them and sent them to the principal's office. Temi told me about this on our way home. "Mom," she said. "The seniors said he was humping her. What does humping mean?" I told her. "Oh, that," she said. "Eew."

I wanted her to feel free to express herself that way, too, so I explained, "They weren't having sex. They are too young."

Being Temi's mother has often meant guiding her and getting my bearings from her at the same time. My protest letter was my first step towards casting off the veil of congeniality in her school. The principal's grins have since been more like winces. The after-hours supervisor is now calling me "Ma'am" instead of "Mrs. Ransome-Kuti," and the librarian no longer asks to read my writings. I was exposed; I have become threatening. The disapproval hurt, but failing to protect Temi wasn't an option, and I was surprisingly relieved in the end: I'd offended good people and I was free to go on offending them.

Temi was more mature than me in the aftermath. At Mass the following Thursday, the principal, as usual, was helping during the service. The last religious experience I needed was to get a blessing from her during communion. "No, I'm not going up there," I said. "Mom-ee," Temi said, and pulled me to my feet. She folded my arms across my chest, and prodded me towards the pulpit. I faced the principal. She gave me the sign of the cross on my forehead. She would have to behave herself, anyway. Plus, the day before was Ash Wednesday, and Lent had just begun.

5.

Perseverance

You're not obligated to win. You're obligated to keep trying to do the best you can every day.

—Marian Wright Edelman

Border Control

Anneli Rufus

I was too old to be an anorexic. That's what it said in the lifestyle-magazine articles and the best-selling books that, in the late eighties, were declaring eating disorders *the* issue of the era, a *cause célèbre*, an issue without which no discussion of modern young American women could be complete. Millions of college students and high school girls, these articles and books announced, were not just dieting but dieting severely, starving, running for miles around school tracks on empty stomachs, bingeing on pizza and M&Ms and then puking it all up. The writers conjured images of sorority-house toilets backed up, clogged with undigested meals. Bulimarexia was a disease, declared the authors of *Dying to Be Thin*. According to *The Golden Cage* and *The Hungry Self*, it was an illness, a bunch of intertwined illnesses, a compulsion, an addiction, a syndrome. It was all about neurotrans-mitters, or zinc deficiency, or daughters' struggles to free themselves from martinet mothers, the literature proclaimed. It was a desperate bid for autonomy, a misguided ploy in which, while you cut the ropes that bound you, you ended up slicing yourself.

Anorexics lost their menses. Bulimics burned holes in their esophagi. The skinniest—having lost their mental hold on reality at seventy, sixty, or forty-five pounds—suffered heart attacks and died in hospital wards devoted entirely to an ever-increasing population of starvers and pukers. The vast majority of this population was middle-class and white, we were told in a scolding tone, as if the pale, stubborn Valley Girl in her nice Nordstrom shoes was willfully mocking the Ethiopians. It was a crisis peculiar to a privileged world, and we were warned to be on guard when our sisters, daughters, friends, or roommates turned down second helpings or dessert—or took too many extra helpings and too much dessert, then hurried off to the restroom. We were warned to listen for that telltale hawk and cough, the gag behind the bathroom door. The second flush. If we loved the suspect, we must watch her closely as she emerged, switching off the bathroom light. Did she wipe her eyes? The corners of her mouth?

They said it was an epidemic.

I was one of the afflicted. One of the hungry who passed bakery windows stiff-backed, like a soldier. One of those who went from daybreak to dusk without eating, a year-round Yom Kippur. And then at dusk, what? A lone burrito, a handful of chips. I was one of those at whose ever-loosening trousers friends frowned, suspecting trickery, which I denied. I was one of the period-less, the dizzy, who saw silvery flashes of light; had I been born five hundred years before, I might have been called a saint, like anorexic Catherine of Siena. I was one of the stubborn. One of the supremely disciplined, the cagey. One of the thin, though not all *that* thin, not quite, and not enough. I wiped the corners of my mouth.

But I was thirty already when those books hit the stands. The girls described therein were *girls*, naive and young, marooned at crucial junctures in their short lives—fighting, at fourteen or twenty, to forge their identities using the only tool and medium they felt was truly theirs: their flesh. Beset by doubts in a brand-new world where females were suddenly free to do whatever, make millions, fly to the moon, make choices, *uh oh*. Bereft of precedent, afraid, girls trembled at the gates.

I scanned the articles and books about the epidemic with that bright electric interest unique to bulimarexics: a stop-start intensity that burns and flares before blurring to sparkly froth before your eyes. They were about me, after all, these tales of wasted opportunity and twig-like wrists. And yet they weren't. The illustrations were always of fluffy, girlish, pink-carpeted rooms with schoolbooks on desks and teddy bears posed on four-poster beds, of adolescent ballet students at the barre.

But I was married. I had strands of silver hair. I had embarked on a career, written books, been on TV; I owned a home. At thirty I stormed up and down the hall in tears when the bathroom scale's marker went the wrong way. I slid my wedding ring up and down on my finger compulsively to reassure myself that it was still too loose, almost loose enough to slip off into the street if I swung my arm. I woke each morning with a silent promise, like a prayer, which I kept: *I will not eat.* I made my husband, whom I loved, alternately furious and fretful.

Never let anyone tell you that bulimarexia doesn't have a good side. It's a regimen, a rule, a mortification, like military service or yoga—demonstrating, like them, strength and dedication, the power of the will. A quest for purity, a mandate rigidly enforced. A law. Border control. Call it sick, but it is a very ordered sickness. Call it self-destructive, but it is a perversely creative destruction. Imagine *kashrut* (those "don't-eat" distinctions laid out in Leviticus: no pigs, clams, crabs, shrimp, scallops, lobsters, mice, chameleons, badgers, weasels, geckoes, eagles, hoopoes, falcons, cormorants, and storks, no milk with meat) stripped of its spiritual wrappings, taken a few strides further. And yet the chooser who decrees, *I will eat this but never that, now but not then*, is making a covenant. Not with a higher power but with herself. That's the problem. That's always the problem. Eating disorders, each case a cult of one, are demonized as selfish. Self-indulgence in the cloak of self-denial. And nobody likes a selfish girl.

In its midst, I never saw it that way. I simply saw it as the way things had to be.

The thing about starving—self-imposed starvation, that is, which is not to be confused with the crueler starvation that comes at the hands of others—is that it sparks euphoria. Spartans flexing on Greek hillsides and Hindu *sadhus* in caves have known it well: a kind of eternal trance in which fleeting thoughts feel profound and happenstance takes on massive significance and becomes kismet. When you're starving, every day is a battle, a siege, a victory: over the body, over the bakery. Who wouldn't want to be able to say, *I've won!* again and again, at the end of every day?

So, still starving at thirty, I was an elder, a veteran; a sibyl, a sage.

Granted, I had entered this realm at the "right" age. During the summer between nineteen and twenty, I worked at a mountain resort. It was there that I sat on my bed at four o'clock one afternoon, pondering the fact that although I was planning to attend a big barbecue that night, I had just devoured a delicious patty melt and a chocolate milkshake. I was full. This presented a problem. At the barbecue, due to begin in an hour, there would be more delicious hamburgers, and beer, and corn, and pie. I *had* to eat them. It seemed a sacrilege, arriving already full at a barbecue as the smoke rose from the coals like silk scarves over the lake. Barbecues embodied the Wild West, the heritage of the state where I lived, the savor of seared meat on yearning, entitled tongues. In the Wild West, hunger was the badge of hard work done and miles made across rough road. It felt wrong, that afternoon, not to be hungry. Shameful. Dishonest. And soft.

So I had a bolt from the blue.

It seemed so logical. What goes in comes out. I had never heard of *vomitoria*, those tiled rooms into which ancient Roman party guests upchucked sensibly to make room for future courses. And it would be years before the media mentioned the new phenomenon of "eating disorders." I didn't know that other nineteen-year-old girls were doing exactly the same thing I was at exactly the same moment, that we were a secret club whose members would never know each other's names. I didn't know there was a name for it. It worked, was all I knew.

And worked again.

Again, again, the succeeding year back at college, and the year after that, beef chow mein, powdered-sugar doughnuts, Rice-a-Roni, torrents of ice cream sliding in, then out. I worked in an ice cream store. I can still taste the Swiss-Orange Chip, back and forth. Hero sandwiches. It worked, worked so well until my boyfriend, when we graduated, told me it was either my bulimarexia or him.

I stayed off the wagon for five years. Doctors say there is a shockingly high recidivist rate for eating disorders, that like an alcoholic the seemingly recovered bulimarexic is haunted by it all her life, whether she acts on her urges or not. She never feels at ease in buffet restaurants. She dreads holiday invitations. After eating certain dishes, namely those with cheese, her eyes will forever dart toward a bathroom door. *There it is.* As to a life raft.

The struggle, sitting so still, telling yourself sternly, *No.* The muscles leap. The middle finger jerks. It knows how easy this would be. The lightness. The relief. The middle finger knows. But *No.*

After five years, when I fell off the wagon, my boyfriend's lectures began again. We lived together now. He begged. He pleaded, asking why. I compromised. Bagels, specific numbers of peanuts and medjool dates. Finite foods, nothing wet or sloppy whose endings and beginnings were unclear. That was proof of my love. He despaired, asking why. I told him why, but it was as if he were deaf.

The reason was my face. I had this problem, see. I have always gained weight in my face first. Eight ounces, a pound—straight to the face. Those who gain weight in their bottoms, hips, or thighs can resort to subterfuge: smocks, skirts. You cannot hide a face. My features, small and naturally delicate, can be overcome like raisins in a massive pudding, sunken, giving me a stupid, squinting look that no hairstyle can sharpen and that is the difference between ugly and not-ugly. People treat you differently when you are ugly. This is inescapably the truth. You think I should not say so. You think this suggests dire things about my self-esteem. But singing "I am beautiful in every single way" a thousand times won't change the truth. I have the photographs to prove it.

So really, as I told him, and continued to say after marrying him, I have to do this because I have a slow metabolism, and this problem with my face. Which is why, at thirty, I was a dates-and-peanuts girl.

How long can somebody live like that, you ask. A long time. You get used to it. My mother's friend Elma kept a framed needlepoint on the wall over her bathroom scale. It said in flowery letters, "You Can Never Be Too Rich or Too Thin." Elma made strudel using Sweet &

Low instead of sugar and then only ever ate a tiny slice, smiling as she served planks of it to her guests. I could have gone on and on, like Elma. I wasn't going to die. Peanuts have protein.

I was sitting on the deck of my house in a bruise-colored twilight, in a trance as windows up and down the street gleamed with a pale golden sheen, when the phone rang. It was summoning me to a hospital at the other end of the state where my father, having just suffered a stroke, lay rigged up to tubes, mumbling gibberish.

It is the same old story. The story nearly everyone, sooner or later, has to tell. I have told it too many times myself. The flight. The wait. The freeway. Hospital, spectacle, debacle. The patient lost already, not quite lost to science as he lives and breathes, stubbornly, but lost to you. Lost to himself. He will not get it back, the doctors admit; he might learn to sit up again, but he will never get back the words and thoughts he has lost. So the nights, the bedside nights. You do not know how this will end—no good way, you know that. You do not eat, those days and nights, but who could eat under such circumstances? He resembles a ghost in his bed, sighing spookily. Three weeks, and then he becomes a ghost for real. And you are left alive. So light that the chill funeral wind blasts your black scarf and almost lifts you off your feet. And then you go home. A member now of *another* club whose members do not greet one another with secret handshakes.

I was suddenly someone with a dead parent, and—bundled in thick sweaters, not speaking, watching a marathon of rented videos— I began to eat.

It isn't what you think. Nothing's what you think, you realize. It wasn't that I was granted some huge cosmic revelation about life and death, e.g., *When you're dead you can't come back so enjoy life!* It was just that I was hungry.

After you have been bulimarexic for many years, not eating does not feel like hunger anymore. You suppress pangs the same way you open your eyes after blinking. Automatically. So the wrenching I felt, watching videos as winter light clung feebly, like weak chicken broth, to the bookshelves was a new and only distantly familiar sensation. The same ache I remembered from way back, from childhood, but fiercer, as if it possessed a voice and fingernails and sinews all its own. It dared me to resist it and I could not.

After you have been bulimarexic for a while, and have been a blithe skeleton, your flesh responds to any slight increase in food with a survivalist determination, manufacturing fat. Ergo, it is the starved who gain weight fastest, given a chance. Ergo, my face . . . And once starved flesh gets going on its own replenishment, all human will lies prostrated before it, helpless. It happens so fast, as if to say *ha ha*.

It was winter, I was thirty, scenes from hospitals and funerals swam past my eyes when I shut them. I was too soft to be a soldier right then, or a Spartan. Someone said, "Join a gym."

She did not say, *Get over it! You are too old to fret about your weight. Who cares? You should be having babies by now anyway and, whoo, when you have kids you'll PACK it on.*

She said, "Gyms work."

They do. Mine did, which seemed awful at first because it was so ordinary. Sure, exercise entails a force of will—even victories and euphoria—but how comparatively plain, amid the cotton shorts and oatmeal-colored lockers. How humdrum in that everyone else is doing it, right in the open, without trickery or cloak-and-dagger sneaking, with no more fanfare than a Walkman flicking on and off.

This is the gym's ultimate power: its dailness. The bored half-smile of the clerk behind the counter, fooling with a pen while watching members glide in and out through the turnstile. What death and starvation taught me was not that there is a God. Nor that each of us has a purpose here on earth. Just that I am nobody special. Starving yourself is a process of believing yourself transcendent, omnipotent, ethereal, exempt from the standard maxims of biology, supreme queen of a sovereignty comprising only your circumference but a domain nevertheless. That is the hardest part to let go, just as on the first day of nursery school you realize with a shock that other four-year-olds are in the world, that among them you hold no sway.

This was torture for me at four, torture again at thirty, descending that pinnacle, being dragged from that trance, forced to follow the laws of gravity while breathing ordinary air.

Baby Baby Baby Please

Judith Newman

When people ask what it was like to be unable to have a baby, I tell them it was like this:

See? It's not so terrible, this blankness. It's clean, quiet, restful. (I wish I could add sound effects to the page; they would be the sound of crickets chirping.) But when you see the space, don't you have the desire to mess it up? Scribble some color, some splodges, a few lines of nonsense? My life was like that. Clean, quiet, sterile. In every sense of the word. I needed to mess it up.

In 1994, I started out as a youngish woman who inexplicably couldn't have a child. If you keep doing infertility treatments long enough, however, you end up being a woman who can't have a baby for a very good reason: you're old. The phrase most often used by specialists is "advanced maternal age." But I appreciated the nurse at one fertility clinic who called it as she saw it: we were the "geriatric mothers."

When I confessed to friends I couldn't have a baby, I discovered everyone was a fertility expert. They all had surefire solutions. Acupuncture! Herbal teas! Cruises! So many people suggested John and I sail to the Bahamas that I began to wonder if cruises weren't actually a form of time travel, where at the end I would wind up with the eggs of an eighteen-year-old.

My own thoughts turned toward moving to a trailer park and drinking heavily. I tried this method, at least the drinking part. Many times. Had I gotten pregnant during those lost weekends, I imagine the child would have been born with a slice of lime in the corner of her mouth. I had heard so many stories of women who conceived after a night of tequila shots that I felt compelled to try the method myself. When you first decide to make a baby, you can't believe your luck. Finally, you and this person you love enough to share a gene pool with can do what nature intended without pills, latex, foams, or goo! It's beautiful. It's almost sacred. But during those years of trying to conceive (or, as it's abbreviated on all the Internet infertility support groups, TTC), one's attitude toward sex evolves in a fairly predictable pattern. It goes something like this:

Fucking

Making love

Having sex

Mating

Performing a science experiment

And at the end, for many of us, that's exactly what it is: a science experiment. And a pricey one, too. Insurance pays for only some of the diagnostic tests and virtually none of the treatments; a one-month round of in-vitro fertilization costs $10,000 to $15,000. The only other medical field similarly shunned by insurance companies is plastic surgery. It's always been interesting to me that in some way, the two are perceived as morally equivalent—medical treatments demanded by vain women obsessed by their DNA, attempting to get their hands on what nature has denied them. Boob jobs and babies, both life's frills. Or as I heard so frequently about infertility: *Hey, it's not cancer.*

When I think back about the years of testing and treatment, the blood sucked out and the drugs plunged in, I always think about the hamsters. There is, you see, a diagnostic procedure known as the "sperm penetration test": a female hamster is super-ovulated with fertility drugs, and a man's sperm is introduced to the eggs to see if they can break through the cell wall. John and I went through the usual jokes—shouldn't he be buying the hamster dinner first? Bringing it flowers, maybe a Habit-Trail? I was surprised when I went to the lab office to discover the technician was not standing there *with* the unfortunate rodent. The sperm, it turns out, is merely sent off to a nearby lab where the hamster is—well, the truth is, I don't know what really happens, and I've never been able to bring myself to find out. Is it sacrificed? Or (as I hope) is it merely subject to incredible mood swings, the result of being put on fertility drugs? Maybe scores of hamsters are shredding boxes of Kleenex to bits right now.

My particular problem seemed not so much to be getting pregnant as *staying* pregnant. After $70,000 worth of testing and treatments, I'd gotten pregnant three times and had three miscarriages. Sometimes, in a perverse attempt to make myself feel better, I'd go to an infertility support group board on the Internet to find people who were even more pathetic than I was:

> *"I have had three miscarriages and two tubal pregnancies. I am divorced, no partner to even have a child with now, and my doctor says it doesn't look good with only one tube and my previous history."*

> *"I spent my Sunday in the ER. They did an internal exam and they they pulled my baby out of my cervix. I stated that I wanted to see it . . . I haven't cried yet."*

> *"Today was the EDD (estimated due date) of my twin babies and it hit me hard. I was supposed to have newborn babies for this Christmas. It just hurts."*

Among my own acquaintances, only one person was cruel—and even then, inadvertently. "Well, you knew you were asking for trouble when you waited this long to have a child," said my agent.

(Did I say agent? I meant ex-agent.)

The vast majority of people tried so hard to be kind, even when they weren't. "Don't worry: You got pregnant, you'll be able to get pregnant again." (This observation was a little wearing by the third miscarriage.) "You need to relax." (Yes, why don't *you* try to relax when you're spending $15,000 you can't afford, to be pumped so full of progesterone you think your head will explode?) My personal favorite: "Well, now you have three angels up in Heaven." Hello, I'm not all that interested in creating little helpers for the Almighty! I'd be much happier to have one small devil down here.

During those years, John of course tried his best to be comforting, but his melancholy nature was no help. "Well, if you can't have children, we can travel," he would say. Finally one day I lost it. "You know what? I've been meaning to tell you this for years," I shrieked. "I don't really *like* to travel! I don't even like to watch The Discovery Channel!"

I was so shaken by the third miscarriage that I waited a year before trying again—a year I could ill afford to waste. As a forty-year-old three-time loser, I was told, I had maybe a 5 percent chance of getting and staying pregnant.

I got and stayed pregnant. I can't honestly say that I was exhilarated and triumphant when I saw two heartbeats. I *can* honestly say I was suffused with a heady combination of disbelief, fear, and nausea, and promptly threw up on the ultrasound technician.

There are more women having their first child over forty than ever before. Most people I know are thrilled for me. But others rail at my selfishness. "You'll be too old to raise them without problems . . . I mean by the time they are thirty you'll be what, seventy?" one woman sneered at me recently. "That's just unnatural."

Unnatural? Maybe. But so's the Sistine Chapel, and no one's complaining about that.

The Cup Is Half-Empty; The Cup Is Half-Full

Autumn Stephens

Choose your battles, they say. An inspiring sentiment, but let's face facts: any engagement of real consequence is damn well going to choose *you*. Three years ago, I was chosen: a routine mammogram led to a less routine biopsy, which revealed that the milk ducts of my right breast were riddled with cancer cells. Those microscopic terrorists, my doctor said (her voice neutral, professional over the phone) were just noodling around in the ducts, harmless as baby newts. But if they ever took it into their pointy little heads to detonate, all hell could break loose. An attack might take place that afternoon, or five years down the road—or never. It was, my doctor said, impossible to say.

An attack now . . . or *never*: that was the irony of the *ductal carcinoma in situ* that, on that sunny July morning in 2001, while my husband was at work, and my children were in daycare, and big, blowsy summer roses were blooming like crazy all over my backyard, I suddenly found myself "fighting."

A preemptive strike, the oncologist said. First we'd try a lumpectomy, and if that didn't work, we'd just cut the damn thing off.

I had never thought of my breasts as the crowning glory of my womanhood. They were not, I regret, rotund and opulent in the classic fashion featured on the innermost pages of *Playboy*. Nor were they small and self-contained in the breezy, athletic, "Look Ma! No bra!" manner that I've always admired. Frankly, they were droopy right from the moment they appeared on my twelve-year-old chest, and, years later, I laughed aloud when a new boyfriend, who had downed a befuddling amount of beer, sighed that they were lovely.

So the surgical proposition that might have struck another woman as cruel or even insane ("we had to destroy the village to save it") scarcely gave me pause. "Losing" a breast, if it came to that, I didn't perceive as an identity-threatening tragedy. But death, if it came to *that*, could really mess with a person's sense of self. I'm no pessimist—I'm a mother, after all. But how could I possibly guess which option fate, left to its own devices, had in mind for me: now . . . or *never*?

I'm a mother, after all. One of my late-life babies was still in diapers, the other barely able to write his name. Tell me, does that sound to you like the ideal time to shuffle off this mortal coil?

A preemptive strike, then.

I have been with (and without, and then with again) my husband, my partner, my life companion, for more than a quarter of a century now. Incomprehensible, it sometimes seems, that the Volvo-driving, tax-paying, insomniac mortgage holder whose ring I wear on my fourth finger was once the gangly, blue-eyed nineteen-year-old who so stirred my soul. That golden California boy, ash blond hair falling lank to his bony shoulder blades; just the kind of hip, pleasantly countercultural-looking boyfriend I had always wanted. Today the man is as bald as a baby, the crown of his head a deep shade of rose. The sun is not as benign as we used to believe; I wish he would remember to wear his hat.

My husband and I met when we both lived in a college co-op known, I blush to admit, as Synergy House. A haven for latter-day hippies and student activists, Synergy listed so outrageously in the direction of political correctness that within its walls, it was—I kid you not—generally considered uncool for one resident to turn down the sexual advances of another. This made it difficult to indulge in the just-the-two-of-us elitism of being a couple. We were all brothers and sisters under the skin, comrades in arms, and in each other's pants, as well. What can I say? It was 1977. It was California. It was a little weird.

Of course, AIDS was an as-yet-unimagined deterrent to lust (or whatever drove us so urgently to mate), but I can't imagine why we weren't all stricken down untimely by syphilis or something. Good luck and antibiotics, I suppose. But in fact, not all of us had such good luck. One young man who lived in Synergy House died of cancer a year after graduation; another, a medical student, overdosed on cocaine.

Back then, the party line was that man-woman differences should not be emphasized. Back then, flirtation—the deliberate, tantalizing exaggeration of difference, through mannerism and adornment—wasn't a prerequisite for sex. Not much *was*, in fact, a prerequisite: we coupled (or, in some cases, tripled or quadrupled) more or less on demand. My husband and I became lovers one early spring night when the lights went out, accidentally on purpose, at a wild party fueled by dope, alcohol, and probably a little LSD. All winter, we had been uneasily circling each other: he was afraid of my sharp tongue; I suspected (not altogether incorrectly, it would turn out) that he was a much nicer person than me. We had never been on a date, never engaged in any of the formal rituals of courtship that previous generations took for granted. But in the dark, we found each other, and while other couples merged and broke apart and merged again in new configurations, we stayed together.

Sometimes I see a middle-aged man—tall and lean like my husband, but with a severe, Abraham Lincoln cast to his face—riding his bicycle down the quiet residential street in Berkeley where my husband and I now live. This man lived in Synergy House with my husband and me, attended the same party of which I was just speaking. What if? What if? It isn't written in stone that things should be as they are.

You know already, don't you, that the easy trade I thought I'd brokered—my saggy, forty-three-year-old breast in return for a shot at a nice, long, quotidian life—didn't go off as smoothly as I had anticipated. Neither my doctors nor I were shocked when the lesser surgical evil, lumpectomy, failed to rout the cancer. No one had promised that it would. What came as a bolt from the blue was the raging post-surgical infection that blindsided me two days later and from which I did, in fact, almost die. The summer of 2001 slipped away as I lay in bed, hooked up to IV meds, too preoccupied with my own condition to notice time passing. It took weeks of those IVs, first at the hospital, then at home, before I was healthy enough to have my breast—what remained of it, anyway—removed.

During this time, the Twin Towers disappeared from the face of the earth.

Sex! It was everything to us when we were young, the entire point of our existence. Back in our more hirsute days—his head, my legs—my husband and I spent most of our time together having sex, squabbling about betrayals real and imagined, and then having more sex. For practically my entire life, I had been an A student. But the spring we got together, I flunked my mandatory senior seminar on The World Food Economy and graduated by the seat of my baggy, olive-green army pants.

Sex! Eventually, we married, then promptly proceeded to betray each other some more, in ways both explicit and ephemeral. Oh, so promptly. For us there was to be no giddy, go-for-broke flush of newlywed euphoria; no honeymoon babies, then, no grand real estate purchases demonstrating our faith in a shared future. So that, when the going got tough, there was nothing concrete to tie us down. Two years to the date from our barefoot beachside wedding, my husband said he wanted a divorce. For weeks afterwards, I felt so shattered that I was sometimes afraid to move, lest I fall apart, so susceptible to rejection that I scarcely dared show my wounded face, my loser's face, to the winner-loving world.

You can get used to anything, though. Here is what my new life was like: lonely, liberating, productive. Quiet, merely quiet, in contrast to the silent screaming despair that had characterized my marriage. And safe: alone, I could not be stabbed in the back, my serenity hijacked by someone else's demons. Over time, I settled deeply into myself. Sometimes, writing on deadline, I didn't leave my apartment for two or three days; barely slept or changed my clothes. This I perceived not as pathology but pleasure, the full expression of a certain driven, antisocial aspect of myself that I tend to experience, or perhaps merely to romanticize, as the "real" me. Because I had red hair and a sarcastic streak, because my stock-in-trade as an author was dangerous, out-of-bounds women, everyone assumed that I had left my husband, not the other way around. This flattering misimpression I did not always correct. Sometimes I believed it myself.

You can get used to anything. When, five years later, my husband and I suddenly and unexpectedly reconciled (a chance meeting, an explosive kiss, déjà vu all over again) I thought hard before consenting to give up my bachelor-girl studio. With some misgivings, I cosigned the loan application for the big gray Victorian in Berkeley that we planned to fill, as soon as possible, with a family.

I was, I admit, swayed by the roses. In that short-lived, fecund season, the backyard of our new home was a riot of sexy, oversized blooms; crimson and tangerine, prom-dress pink, the luxurious, creamy off-white of expensive lingerie. Only after closing the deal did we discover that our slice of jointly owned real estate lies directly beneath the flight pattern for aircraft headed to and from the Oakland International Airport. Jet trails sear the sky, a constant reminder, and of course no one likes to hear that distant, window rattling rumble which might signify a Boeing 747 passing overhead, or an earthquake, or the end of the world.

But still, there were the roses.

And so it came to pass that a few years later, I was sitting one morning on the front porch of that well-weathered house, cradling a newborn in my arms. My husband (for such he was again, in the legal sense) and our older son, now a toddler, were frolicking on the sidewalk, just a few feet away. At long last: Snapshot of a Happy Family. (Although a more penetrating portrait would have revealed how mistrust still constricted the wife's heart, how the husband bloodied his inner cheek with his teeth, biting back his words.)

Sometimes danger takes you unaware, but other times, it's easy enough to foresee. As I watched, idly at first, then with stiff-spined attention, a large U-Haul started to pull into the unoccupied parking space in front of our house. The truck was moving too fast, the driver not fully in control. So, then, the inevitable collision, the truck slamming headlong into a tall carob tree that stood at the edge of our property. Severed branches flew through the air, one of them taking down a power line that sputtered wildly as it plummeted to the ground. A shower of electrical sparks strafed the porch as, screaming, I scrambled with the baby for the uncertain safety of the house.

That day, I foresaw danger, but to what avail? There was nothing I could have done to stop the inexorable forward motion of that truck, just as in those nightmares where you discover, as the monster or the tsunami or the ax murderer closes in, that you can't run or remember how to scream. Reconciling with my husband felt like that, at first. A lot of things feel like that. No wonder we humans are so wary of the world, and of each other. Our natural habitat is in harm's way.

You hear a lot about "reconstruction" when you're being treated for breast cancer. The term always makes me think of the Civil War; blood-soaked battlefields, the doomed effort to heal and move on while the smell of death still hangs in the air. But of course that's not what the plastic surgeons have in mind when they say how swell you're going to look. "You've always wanted a boob job," my sister joked, though that wasn't entirely true—what I'd wanted was for nature to provide me with a perky pair, not for my insurance company to buy me one. In any event, reconstruction was not an option for me. For medical reasons. And for other reasons.

For better or worse, I have seldom in my life been able to summon—much less sustain—a viable sense of femininity. Branded by youthful ideology, I suspect, although it's obvious—all those lip-sticked matrons in crisp capris at the supermarket—that many escaped unmarked. In any event, the precise meaning of femininity, that exquisitely subjective construct, eludes me: I probably couldn't come up with a definition if you put a gun to my head. I can say only that I find it telling that "femininity" can't stand on its own two feet, that it's irrelevant outside of the context of its relationship with "masculinity," its opposite number, its codependent, its mate. Whatever the F-word may mean, though, I am certain that a matched set of mammaries doesn't define it.

Was it painful? In the big-picture sense, the question is moot, the same way that the distant agony of labor, as you wave your kindergartner off to school, is entirely beside the point. I was lucky, compared to many. No radiation, no chemo. Didn't look sensational, afterwards, in a swimsuit, but I got to keep my hair. And, of course, I'm alive. Not history, not yet. The manner and hour of my death—as far as I know, anyway—yet to be determined.

And yet: blood, wound, scar. I had willingly consented to the surgery, but on a visceral level, I perceived these bodily alterations as proof of malevolent assault. From fever and from fear (for myself, for the world), my appetite had vanished; I weighed the same as I had in sixth grade. Sometimes, thinking of how fragile I looked and felt, the word "feminine" did indeed float into my mind. A bud on a severed branch. I wasn't in much physical distress. I took every last Codeine that the surgeon prescribed.

Even now, noticing a newly patched portion of a city street, the dark asphalt scar, I am acutely aware of my upper chest. That flat, empty surface where I sometimes feel tingling and sometimes feel pain, but where most of the time I feel nothing.

But my husband, let's not forget about my husband. For of course this is not (much as I might have liked, at times, for it to be) my history alone. My "fight" alone. And during the time that I am speaking of, it could not escape my captive attention how much my husband, my embattled husband, cared for me. The man cared—specifically and pragmatically—for me. With his own two hands, he bandaged the nothingness, ground zero, that I did not want to see, not yet, not yet. Uncomplainingly drained the plastic tubing that drew pus and blood from my chest; matter-of-factly measured that foul fluid in a cup and recorded its quantity, as the surgeon had blithely, sadistically ordered us to do. And over and over, the ritual of scrubbing skin, smoothing the latex gloves over his familiar, competent hands, inserting the IV into my tense but upturned arm. Over and over, until finally my apprehension subsided, and I looked up with unadulterated trust into his tired but still-blue eyes.

There are easier ways to heal a marriage than by having cancer. But that is how it was for us. I was ill, and my husband offered me sustenance and compassion, which are, I see now, other words for love. My husband offered me sustenance and compassion, and I did not turn away.

Like many women my age, I lament that my libido is not what it once was. I'm preoccupied with the children, or work, or simply weary, thinking of nothing except how much I would like to be asleep. The last thing I want to do is to move, or to be moved. Nor do missing body parts tend to have an aphrodisiac effect on the flickering spark of midlife sex drive. I'm speaking strictly for myself here; my husband doesn't seem to mind. Make no mistake: if we were to divorce again, it would be from lack of sex, not lack of breasts.

But you're not thinking, are you, that I should be grateful that my husband still finds me alluring, that he cleaves to my disfigured side? I concede that it's not the ideal denouement, to forsake all others for someone who turns out, in the end, to be so nakedly flawed. Yet haven't we all done precisely that, every one of us who has ever vowed fidelity to another human, another imperfect human being? Believe me, if I could, I'd spread myself out on the sheets like a lush landscape of sensual delights, the full complement, everything a lover could desire. But I do what I can, I make a sporadic effort, and it is true that we are close to each other afterwards. He wraps his arm around my shoulder, and I attempt to amuse him, or at least to speak of topics other than our boys' behavior and tasks that remain to be done.

One afternoon last summer, my then three-year-old and I were strolling down the sidewalk, pausing, as we do, to examine the many objects of interest—pebbles, ants, cigarette butts—that we found along the way. That day we were truly in luck, or so it seemed: a gorgeous trumpet flower, orange and mauve and, indeed, somewhat resembling a miniature musical instrument, had fallen from the vine. But when my happy boy held up the blossom for me to admire, we suddenly saw that the underside was mottled and brown. Consternation wrestled with determination on his young face. "Here, Mommy," he said, his voice quavering as he handed me the damaged flower. "Can we pretend it's perfect?"

In pretending, we sometimes forget. But in pretending, we also remember. Naked before the mirror, I marvel at the sight of my ribs, now so cleanly articulated. Mine (or half mine, anyway) is the bony, unembellished torso of a teenage boy, like that of my husband at nineteen, when sex was the sticky glue that bonded us, blurring the boundaries so that it was impossible to tell where one of our bodies stopped, where the other began. But now, of course, it's obvious which is mine. Mine is the one with the thin pink scar running northeast to southwest, pointing toward my heart.

What to Save

Anne Burt

Accuse not Nature: she hath done her part;
Do thou but thine.

—John Milton, *Paradise Lost*

"The rhododendrons have *got* to go," said Barbara as she stood in my front yard, waving in disgust at the massive forest around us. In blooming season, the purple blossoms run all the way up to the master bedroom window on the second floor. The shutters were painted purple to match the flowers. I had hired Barbara, a decorator, to turn my hundred-year-old house from a parade of papers, books, and college-dorm-room-era clutter into a Charming Colonial Revival on a Desirable Enclave in Move-In Condition. I had made the harrowing decision to separate from my husband; now I had to sell the house as part of the divorce agreement and move somewhere more affordable with my daughter, Tessa.

"The rhododendrons are famous," I told Barbara. "Everyone calls this the rhododendron house."

"Well, they look like shit," she answered. "Chop them down and I guarantee you'll get ten percent over asking price." Barbara was a fifty-something woman with dyed black hair, severely arched eyebrows, and a crust of makeup so deep it almost made her multi-carat diamond earrings recede. She had sold a dozen houses at a profit and even been through a divorce herself. I paid her $150 an hour, borrowed from my parents as an advance against the sale of my house. She told me where to put the couch, how to fold my towels, and what to dig up out of the ground.

"But I love the rhododendrons," I protested. "I'll weed them. I'll make them look good."

"Listen to me," Barbara continued. "This isn't about decorating your dream house. It's about selling the dream of this house to someone else. You want to project an image. A scraggly, overgrown stick forest isn't part of it."

I was no gardener. Five years earlier, when Wayne and I moved in, nothing had scared me more than the rhododendrons. Moving day was a blissful autumn afternoon. Kids on bicycles yelled from the street, hovered over by watchful parents and the sheltering rooftops of eclectic, turn-of-the-century houses.

"You have to keep the rhododendrons looking good," said a well-meaning neighbor. "When they bloom in the spring, your house is a stop for the ladies on the garden tours."

We did nothing. I couldn't bring myself to touch the rhododendrons—they seemed so much more important than me. A longtime city dweller, I had no concept of the ground. The only growing thing I had ever owned was a small houseplant with dark green, rubbery leaves shaped like hearts, and tendrils that curled as it grew. I never bothered to learn its genus, or species, or even its common, plant-store name. The plant predated my marriage; it grew anywhere, wilting or unfurling depending on whether I bothered to water it in a given week. I treated it with benign neglect for a dozen years, yet remained committed to trundling it in its pretty rattan basket from apartment to apartment to house in the suburbs surrounded by rhododendrons.

When the first lavender shimmer of flower broke through a tight green bud the following May, we were stunned. The rhododendrons didn't seem to care that the real owners had abandoned them. Indifferent to our shock, the blossoms popcorned forth until a week later, the blaze of purple reached well into the sky. The afore-promised garden tours brought white-haired ladies in Mephisto walking shoes.

Evenings, Wayne and I stood together under the rhodies, transforming our view of the world through a green and purple kaleidoscope. I was pregnant; the flowers were riotously beautiful. We held hands and rhapsodized about how life was just *happening* all around us and inside us.

As the days grew longer and warmer, the petals began to drop on our front lawn. Before long, the ground radiated more purple than the sky. That's when I started to notice the weeds. Bright green growth flashed amidst the knotted brown rhodie trunks. The purple blanket was gone, replaced by a haze of stalks that looked unnaturally fresh and vibrant in contrast to the rhodies' duller gray-green leaves. I peeked out from behind the window. Some of the weeds had lacy leaves; a few even had delicate white flowers.

I panicked. Nobody who deserved to own big rhododendrons visited by garden tour ladies would ever let the weeds grow out of control.

Wayne was even more useless than me at garden care, so the dirty work would be done by me or no one. But I found myself entangled in a moral dilemma: weeding seemed to be the most fundamental act of colonialist aggression. A baby was growing inside of me; how could I kill weeds? Wasn't the best decision to leave the weeds and flowers to their Darwinian fate? I popped my prenatal vitamin and watered my little houseplant. I did not weed.

By late summer, the excess of life unchecked crept everywhere. My pregnant belly grew bigger daily, and the weeds peeked over the front porch railing. And then a ferocious windstorm felled a forty-foot oak on the sidewalk in front of our yard. I heard the crack—which sounded as if someone said the word "crack"—from my attic office, and waddled down to see what happened. The giant tree splayed across the front right side of our property, missing our house by a foot. Half of the rhododendron system was smashed. I watched from the porch while town emergency crews rushed to the scene with police tape and power saws and backhoes.

We hired a tree company to pluck and prune the rhodies after the crash.

"Please save as much as you can," I begged the tree expert. "They've always been here. The garden tours come."

I wrote the expert a check, shook his hand, and decided to let him take care of the weeds from then on too. He showed me photos of his twins, a boy and a girl, newly born. I touched my own pregnant stomach, cooed and sighed appropriately.

But with half of the rhodies' hundred-year growth gone and the remaining bushes gangly and bare, that spring was the last of the garden tours. I swore that once my daughter was older, I'd turn my attention to these rhododendrons and nurture them back to their former glory. Already, new growth was peeking out from between the crooked, naked old branches.

Now, three years later, I was about to sell the house, and the rhododendrons still looked bedraggled. Since Tessa's birth—and the subsequent failure of my marriage—my time had been spent tending to our lives, not our plants. I had to let the tree service go because I could no longer afford it. The weeds swallowed the rhododendrons, jungly and fierce.

"You have to decide whether to cut those rhododendrons down or try to shape them up," Barbara chastised me. "The house goes on the market in six weeks."

August heat, afternoon haze. I didn't even know what tools to use. I had a little fork-like digger thing and a spoon-like shovel thing Wayne and I once bought in an experimental foray to a plant store: so armed, I took a deep breath and plunged into the thicket.

The first weed I saw was my height, with a stalk thick as my arm, and pea-green, oblong leaves. I looked at the fork and spoon, then back up at this creation. I dropped the fork and spoon in the dirt, crouched on my heels, and grabbed the stalk in both hands. I started to pull.

I didn't want to know what kind of weed I had by the throat; to name your enemy is to give it power. But also, to name the weed would remind me that it, in some cosmic picture, was on equal terms with the rhododendrons. I was the intruder here, not the weed. Weed and rhodies were growing—I lumbered in with my fork and spoon, playing God, choosing death for some, life for others.

The dark, wet earth gave way; a seismic shift threw me back onto the ground, weed in my grip. I looked at the broken root system before me. The sight was staggering. The stalk continued with a bulbous white knob caked in dirt, with tiny brown hair-like growths dotting its surface. From the knob, long tentacles, brown and white, dangled helplessly. A moment ago they had probed the ground for minerals. Now they were useless, thanks to my marauding hands.

As I stared at the weed, I wondered what I had done. I felt neither triumphant nor cleansed and cleansing, but disgusted and vaguely sickened. But now I had started. Just as inertia and fear kept me in my house staring out the window before I entered the thicket, the mere fact that I'd already ruined one weed convinced me that I should ruin the rest. I grabbed another and braced myself with my heels in the earth. As the pile of four-, five-, six-foot-long stalks accumulated behind me, I began to crave the moment when each weed would release its grip on the world. My daughter was with her father; I had the whole day to myself. I weeded well into dark.

The next morning I walked outside, barefoot, holding my fresh mug of coffee, to survey my work. I had filled twelve giant garbage bags with weeds and sticks. More piles lay like haystacks on the lawn, ready for bagging. And the rhododendrons themselves rose free and clear, hard buds clenched fist-like among the oblong leaves, already present and waiting for next May to come and force them open to the sun.

"Wow," said a neighbor walking her dog past my house. "The rhododendrons look amazing."

I stood and watched them for a long time, saw the sun grow hotter on the fruits of my labor. Then I turned back to go inside and picked up the phone to call Barbara.

"Cut them down," I said.

A garden crew arrived that afternoon. Barbara had chrysanthemums planted over the gaping earth in front of the house; the flowers opened just in time for the realtors' open house in September. I got ten percent over asking price.

I'm back to renting again; my little houseplant in its rattan basket is still with me. Now my daughter is with me too—my beautiful, blue-eyed, brilliant Tessa. Sometimes I lie with her in bed when she's asleep, feel the top of her head jammed under my chin. My tears wet her pillow because I don't know—maybe I'll never know—if she has a mother who understands what to save and what to throw away.

Legends: The Daughter

Edwidge Danticat

I

Let me tell you now the story of all that happened to me in your absence, the story of my life while you were gone.

Until very recently, I had only few memories of my childhood with you. Fragments of my life between my birth and the time you left. My first memory is of you sitting with me in the two room concrete house where we lived, up in the hills of Bel-Air, that house crowded in between so many others on a slope of shacks overlooking Port-au-Prince harbor. Between our house and the harbor was the cathedral and the Iron Market, and the people who packed themselves along the street each day like a constant carnival parade, buying and selling things, taking their children to school, living it seemed a waiting dance. Perhaps I thought they were waiting because we were waiting. Waiting for my father who had left for New York a year before to send us money, letters, and cassettes from across the sea. From our house, we could always see the sea and the large ships that docked at the port with provisions that were never coming for us. Sometimes there would be rumors that the ships were also bringing armies from abroad to rescue not just us, but the whole country from the president, the dictator, the tyrant who was ruling us. But of course, I didn't know all that then. All I knew was you and the two-room concrete house and you rushing back and forth between the small cooking space in the back where you fanned charcoal and dried sticks to make three meals a day and then sat on your rag-padded mattress, on the bed with the squeaky springs to sew cloth that people brought to you into dresses. I remember you making matching dresses for us, always buying a little extra cloth, so that when you made yourself a dress, you made one for me too. And I remember people smiling and admiring us in those dresses and I remember feeling like I was so intricately a part of you in those dresses, like your arm or your leg, or even your heart.

I remember the day you took me to school for the first time. I was three years old. That morning, my first day of school, we kneeled down before your bed, a bed that I slept in with you at night; we both kneeled there in front of the bed and you prayed. I remember the intensity in your voice, the perspiration rolling down your face, your voice growing louder and louder as you prayed. "I am trusting you, Jesus, with her in your care," you said, "I am trusting you to open her mind. I am trusting you to keep all jealous eyes off her." You were sobbing at the end of the prayer, as you always do when you pray so intently, as you still do when you pray so intently. And I was sobbing too, not wanting to leave you to spend my days with strangers.

I remember people calling greetings to us as we walked out of the house on my first day of school, our skipping to avoid the mud spots in the narrow alley between the houses. You carried my school bag, inside which was a notebook, two overly sharpened pencils, and a small bag of grilled peanuts for a recess snack. Someone who had been washing clothes in front of her house almost covered us with a basin of dark soapy water, which she was discarding on the street. You did not get mad as no harm was done.

Later you would tell me that on this day going to school, this was the first time our dresses were of different colors. I was wearing my plaid brown uniform with CEP (Collège Elliott Pierre) carefully embroidered on the left pocket. I had seen you sewing that uniform and embroidering those initials on the pocket, but never thought that you were doing it for me.

We arrived late at the school. The other children were already on line with their right hands held out, their faces following the black and red flag up a pole, while they sang the national anthem in unison, "*Marchons unis, let's walk together, marchons unis.*" The only person I wanted to walk together with at that point was you.

In the school's main office, we could still hear the street noises outside, people chanting the prices of mangoes, bananas, and eggs. This was our real life. These were our people. And even then I had a feeling that I was taking the first step in leaving them behind.

The secretary at the school's registration office said that I would be in Room Three. I remember Room Three because three was my age. You were to leave, the secretary told you; she would take me to the class. This was when I began screaming at the top of my voice. You knotted up your face and shot me a poisoned glance: behave yourself or suffer a tap on your bottom. I would have preferred a hundred taps to being taken away from you, so I screamed until my throat ached.

The secretary told you to leave or I would never stop screaming. I didn't think you would walk out, but you did. You walked backwards out the door and practically ran out of the school. It worked. As soon as you left I stopped screaming. What would be the use now? The secretary seemed immune to my pain; she grabbed me by the elbow and dragged me to Room Three. I didn't want the other children to think I was more infantile than they, so I wiped my face and stopped crying as we walked into the classroom.

My teacher was beautiful. She was plump and tall and chocolate-skinned. She had perfectly manicured long nails. I remember her so well, because I was contrasting her to you. I thought how perfect her hair was, in a bob along the sides of her made-up face, the way you could only look on Sundays and special occasions, she could afford to look all the time. She assigned me a seat in the front row and called me "Danticat," by my last name; no one had ever called me by my last name before. She asked me to take out my notebook. We were going to begin our education by learning to write lower and upper-case "A" in between the perfect parallel lines of our notebooks.

The A was difficult for me to copy as modeled on the board. After several tries, the teacher tapped me on the knuckle with a ruler and told me I had a thick skull.

I remember recess. Some of the other children bought ice cream from the vendors in the schoolyard. You did not believe that children should carry money, so I ate the peanuts you had already bought for me and placed in my school bag.

I don't remember the rest of the day. I only remember the homework that night. You took me to my cousin Marie, the nurse, and asked her to help me with my homework, which was not only to write A's but also the rest of the alphabet. My cousin Marie, the nurse, made me do this several times on a piece of scrap paper and then urged me to copy the alphabet into my school notebook. I copied the alphabet backwards from W to A; my cousin Marie, the nurse, told me I had a thick skull.

I remember feeling hungry when I came back from Marie's. You were late with supper and told me that you would soon have it cooked, *sou de chèz*, literally "on two chairs." This was my first lesson on the figurative power of our language, our Kreyòl. I later learned that your *sou de chèz* meant "real fast." But the image was already carved into my brains: Manman (you) cooking on two chairs; it seemed impossibly beautiful.

I became the star pupil in the class that first year; it turned out I didn't have a thick skull after all. You were proud to go to the school on Friday afternoons to collect my weekly grade reports. Often I was first or second in my class and you were happy. You would reward me by letting me have a piece of hardened molasses, which we called *rapadou*. You took me to the photo studio downtown to take pictures in my school uniform to send to my father in New York.

I never knew how much you missed my father and how much you worried that he might never come back for you. When he left for New York, he had promised to return and take us with him to the United States. Were you scared then that he would forget his promises? Were you afraid that he would stop loving you?

There was no one to tell any of this to. Least of all me. I later learned that my father's family, who lived nearby, did not like you. They didn't think my father should have married you. You had been raised Catholic and his family was Baptist. They considered these irreconcilable differences. This left you so desolate in the city, far away from your own town, your own mother and sisters. How many nights did you lie there next to me on that squeaky metal bed and cry while I was asleep?

Soon, my father did send for you. I don't know when the word came or when your papers came, but you seemed happier. You started giving away your things, the spotless white sheets you kept hidden under the bed for a sick day, you gave to my cousin Marie, the nurse, as a reward for helping me with my homework. You made me more dresses. You were like a factory of dresses. You made me dresses that were too big for me. Little did I know that you were making me dresses to wear into the future, when you were gone.

When the day came for you to leave, I thought that I was leaving too. We drove with my father's brother, my uncle Joseph, to the airport and I sat on your lap. Everyone was silent, as I remember it; nothing was said. When we got to the airport, you handed over your bags to the airplane people and the two of us started for the gate. Tears gathered in your eyes, but I didn't realize that the tears were for me. I thought you were going to miss your mother and your sisters who had not been able to come see you off at the airport.

When it was finally time for you to get on the plane, my uncle started tugging at me. I thought he wanted to say a final goodbye. It was getting late and you had to go. I threw both my arms around you and made you unable to move. My uncle was now yanking at me, trying to peel me off your body.

In my screams that day, I heard the echoes of my first day at school. You ran to the plane. I don't remember you turning back again for a final glance.

Later, at fifteen years old, in New York, I would holler at you during a fight, declaring that I had to mother myself at a young age. I had to toughen up, to be brave, even take care of others because you were not there. I remember you calmly muttering, "Do you think it was easy for me?"

A year ago, I met a young woman who had been spared that scene at the airport during her own mother's departure from Haiti.

She was five when her mother left. Her mother had reasoned that her daughter would not be able to handle seeing her go. So the mother left for the airport while the daughter was asleep. When the daughter woke up, her aunt, in whose care she had been left, told her that her mother was *lòt bò dlo*, on the other side of the waters. Having previously heard her family members use that same figurative expression to say that someone had passed over into the next world, the daughter had assumed that her mother had died. When her mother would send her letters and cassettes from New York, the daughter would not open them, thinking that all the phone calls, the presents, the money that came to her from across the waters was only an elaborate ruse to console an orphan. Even when she was finally reunited with her mother in New York some seven years later, she never really believed that this was her real mother. She was twenty-two when we spoke and still could not erase all traces of doubts from her mind that the woman she called "Manman" was really her mother.

Perhaps it was good that I was able to see you leave. Perhaps it was better that I formed in my mind what it was to grieve. Perhaps it was best for me to first doubt and then slowly begin to trust that I would see you again.

II

You were pregnant very soon after arriving in the United States. Early on in your pregnancy, you worked in a factory. And since you had come to New York on a tourist visa and had no permit to work, you were arrested in a factory raid and put in immigration jail. Often I am forced in my own head to assign words to your silences, things that I imagine you might have said, things that you might say, lumping them together with the little you have been able to say. But still I respect your caution. I respect your reserve. I learned this story about your being in jail when I was sixteen years old, listening to a sermon in our church in Brooklyn, a sermon preached by our minister, Reverend Phylius Nicolas. During the sermon, Reverend Nicolas used yours and Papi's example of being separated for two years and then your coming to the United States finally and then being arrested and going to jail while pregnant. According to Reverend Nicolas' sermon, while you were in jail, my father exhausted all his means trying to get you out and went to a lawyer who told him to divorce you while you were still in jail, marry an American citizen, get citizenship, and then marry you again. The lawyer, it seemed, was thinking long term, but not about how to get you out of jail.

Since Papi refused to do any of these things, I don't know how you finally got out of jail, but when you did, you were sick for a while and a bit worried that your pregnancy had been compromised. It was. My brother Kelly was born seven months later with his right forearm missing and the doctor said that it was perhaps because you'd had some shock early on in your pregnancy.

Did they beat you in jail?

How did you pass the time?

Did you think of me?

You said later that you dreamed of telling me stories every day when you got up and every night before you went to sleep—stories of things to watch out for: scary things in the night, scary things in the day, people not to talk to. You dreamed of telling me moral, historical, family tales that you thought I would eventually forget. I would not be hurt if while you were jailed, you only thought of stories for my brother Kelly, of tales to keep him alive.

III

You were gone eight years from my life. In that time, my dresses matched no one's. People told me stories, lots and lots of stories, but none of them were tailor-made for me. They were told generally into the night, to a crowd of us, sitting at the feet of the elders in our lives. (*"Krik? Krak!"*) My uncle Joseph's mother-in-law, my aunt Denise's mother, Granmè Mélina, told stories from her rocker, while I braided her hair. When I visited your mother, Granmè Grace in Léogane, she told stories too. I kept wishing that she would tell stories of how you were when you were a little girl, but she never did. She too had a penchant for history, Granmè Grace did; she told me about the French generals who, during colonial times, had always been thinking of new ways to kill our people. She told me that American soldiers, Marines, had taken over our country for nineteen years before they went off to fight World War II, soldiers whose boots coming down a dirt road sounded like the mythical three-legged horse Galipòt, who would mistake humans for his missing fourth leg and chase them down in the night, trying to claim something he believed to be not only his, but part of him. It was her daughter, your sister, my aunt, also named Grace who told me that you were named Rose after Saint Rose de Lima, patroness of Léogane, patroness of the Caribbean who was so beautiful that no one could keep their eyes off her, so to keep vanity and admirers at bay she sanded her face with peppers and blistered her perfect complexion. Saint Rose had died young, at thirty-one.

You seemed so angry when I officially changed my name to Rosa Edwidge Danticat the day I became a naturalized United States citizen at eighteen. It was a last-minute decision quickly determined in a Brooklyn courthouse while waiting on line to officially pledge allegiance to a new world. I added "Rosa" to my first name to honor you or at least to try, in my own mind, to alleviate the sting of the time that you had spent in immigration jail.

While you were gone, even when I was not in physical danger, I always thought I would die. I never expected to grow up to be an adult, a *gran moun*, a big person like you. Perhaps this had to do with my uncle Joseph and Granmè Mélina.

My uncle Joseph, who you left me with, was a minister of a church where he was often called on to preside over funerals. He, his wife, and I always went to all the funerals. I went to each and every one of those funerals in the knee-high white ruffled dress that you had sent for me, the one that looks like a wedding dress, except it was short and for a little girl. The funerals would always start out in Bel-Air and end up in a march through the city towards the cemetery, with the bereaved wailing in front of the hearse and a joyous symphonic march of drums and trumpets trailing behind the hearse. How confused the dead must have been, I remember thinking then, with both joy and sorrow at either end of their extremities

While you were gone, my uncle Joseph got cancer. Before he was a minister, he had smoked for some twenty-five odd years and even after he had repented, it all caught up with him. His voice grew more and more hoarse until one day he couldn't preach, and then the next day he couldn't speak. He had to go outside of the capital, to an American hospital in a southern province to be treated for this illness and there they told him he had throat cancer. When he was gone, after a week of his absence, I went with my aunt Denise to a radio station to make a general announcement for him to send news home from the hospital. You tell this story now with pride as if you had been there. "Imagine my daughter," you say, "ten years old, going on the radio to declare, 'Reverend Joseph Danticat, please send word home, your family is worried about you.'" You tell this story now as if you had been there: two days later, my uncle Joseph sent an open telegraph over the same radio station to say that he had gotten the message and that he would be home soon.

While you were gone, my uncle Joseph went to the United States to be operated on for cancer. He was with you a month while being treated.

I tell this story now as if I had been there. One night while my uncle Joseph was with you in New York, his throat collapsed completely on him and closed down his larynx as well as his windpipe. They had to drill a hole into his throat before he could reach the hospital to have his larynx removed forever, his voice taken away permanently.

I can't remember now, what my uncle Joseph's voice sounded like when it wasn't hoarse with cancer or when it wasn't the robotics box that he uses now to speak. Can you? Do you want to? For it had been that same voice which had pronounced you unworthy of my father so many years ago.

While my uncle Joseph was in New York with you, the structure of our family fell apart in Port-au-Prince. Somehow, the funds you and Papi sent for our food didn't reach us at all. One Sunday, I remember my aunt Denise asking us all to collect bottles around the house to sell so we could buy food to eat. There were many days when all we had was sugared water and bread.

When my uncle Joseph came back from his operation in New York, I was glued to his side. I felt maternal towards him, if ever I have felt maternal towards anyone. I was always a few feet from him, reading the notepad, where he scribbled his greetings, kind words, and orders. I learned how to read his lips, both when he had and when he didn't have his dentures in his mouth.

While you were gone, I wrote you with many requests, for dolls and jewelry that never came. Later you told me that you had sent me a four foot tall doll, gold loop earrings, a heart-shaped pendant, and a gold chain. All of this was stolen by the people given to deliver them to me. (I never learned who those people were.) One wish that was realized was when I asked you to send me a typewriter and you did, a small manual typewriter with black and red ribbons.

I used my typewriter to write letters for my uncle Joseph, and all the people in the neighborhood who needed letters written. They would dictate their most intimate thoughts, forgetting I was only ten years old.

While you were gone, I grew up much faster than you would have liked. I was too comfortable with death, thinking of it, as Saint Augustine had said, as a door—a festive one at that—into another room. My uncle Joseph was counting on me a great deal for his needs of speech: he would take me to the bank, the notary, every official public place where he had to be. My days of being a child were over.

While you were gone, Granmè Mélina died. She was over ninety years old. She had been complaining of *doulè*, body pains, but all the old people I knew did. I brought her coffee to her in bed the morning that she died. When I went in there, she was still. I took a small mirror from her night table and held it in front of her nose. I had seen my aunt Denise do this before when Granmè Mélina had just been sleeping. I put the mirror in front of her nose and saw no fog rise to the surface of the glass. Her eyes were wide open so I closed them and sat there for a long time on the floor next to her bed, watching her face.

I imagine now how we might have made an interesting painting, Granmè Mélina and me that day, two generations apart, separated by life and death. For a long time I believed I was rescued from death by my aunt Denise walking into the room to discover that she was now motherless.

I remember too when your own mother, Granmè Grace, died. It was a month after I had officially added Rosa to my name. You had to go to Haiti for the funeral and when you came back, all I could do was ask if you cried. I remember your sucking your teeth at me, asking incredulously, "Did I cry?" I had only wondered if you would cry because you spent so much time away from your mother. Between the time that you left Haiti to come live in New York and the time that she died, you had only seen each other once in twelve years. I didn't realize then that this long absence would have compounded rather than relieved your grief.

While you were gone, I had my first menstruation. I didn't tell anyone because I was ashamed. My aunt Denise did not give me a set of menstrual rags, like she had all the other girls in the house, because I had not gone to her to ask. Perhaps I would have been ashamed to tell you about my menstruation too, but maybe you would have handled it differently.

While you were gone, I filled my void of stories by reading. I read a set of books given to me by my uncle as a reward for helping him communicate with the world. They were the stories of a mischievous girl named Madeline, who lived in France. France seemed as far away as the United States, but, my uncle Joseph thought, more pleasant.

Perhaps it was because it was the place where he finally lost his speech, but my uncle Joseph was a bit afraid of the United States. When my papers finally came for me to go off to New York to be with you and Papi, my uncle Joseph mouthed, "Good luck; don't lose yourself in New York."

I tried to write of my fears about going to New York on the type-writer you sent me, making myself a list of all that had happened to me while you were gone. Writing this now is only now a smaller effort at recreating this document, lost so long ago.

IV

I remember when I first saw you at the airport in New York. I was twelve years old. I had never thought that it would be so, but we were like strangers. You were heavier, just weary-looking, standing there next to my father who was sprinting towards me. Perhaps you were glued to your spot by some fixed memory, another airport, another country.

I was lucky that I could not remember my father's departure. It was our curse that I remembered yours, every vivid second of it, as if it were just then playing on a movie screen in front of both of us.

V

I don't think you and I have been together alone, just the two of us, for any extended period of time since Haiti, since before I went to school that day. Recently when we took a trip to Miami, me to attend the Miami Book Fair and you to visit some relatives, I was so angry at the airline that we did not get to sit together. How could they have known how precious this little time was for me?

I was going to pry you for your stories, ask you to tell me all about your life, demand that you fill in all the gaps: the factory, the jobs, looking after other people's children. But I didn't ask you any-thing. Instead I found it was enough, just sharing a hotel room with you, lying awake in the dark at night to listen to you snore and whis-per incomprehensible sentences in your sleep, like I do.

There was only one frightening moment during the trip, when I woke up the last morning in the hotel room and you were gone. I can't tell you how distraught I was after looking all over the hotel and not finding you. The half hour that I waited for you to come back seemed eternal, forcing me to imagine the worst, which I realized just then alone in that hotel room, I had spent my whole childhood fearing, the fact that I might never see you again.

When you came back, I almost wanted to yell at you for taking your solitary stroll along a nearby highway, but if I had yelled, and if I did yell, it was because the possibility was too unbearable to revisit again. But these days, as we both get older, I find it inevitable not to think about these things.

VI

This year, I am living away from home, forty minutes from where you live. It has been four months now since we came back from Florida, two months since you fell down the stairs in your house in Brooklyn and had to be rushed to the hospital. I feel guilty that I was in Chicago on a book tour and could not instantly rush to your side. When I called you, you assured me that you were okay. There was nothing to worry about; your foot just slipped and you went tumbling. You even laughed when you said this, which worried me. Would your taking this so lightly mean that you would not take precautions and go tumbling again?

The other day, while you and I were limping up these same stairs in the house, you still a bit sore from the fall and me sore from an attempt at weightlifting, my youngest brother, Karl, glanced down at both of us from the top of the steps and joked, "Look at those two old ladies."

It is no cliché, that I am definitely beginning to see your face in mine when I look in the mirror.

One thing I don't think you know. In your absence, there were times when I considered my age in what I call "Manman years," subtracting from my birthdays the time I spent apart from you. In Manman years, I am still only twenty-three years old (instead of thirty-one, my real age). At twenty-two, you were still unscarred from agonizing separations, the arrest, the limbo of living in but never being completely part of a new world.

Yes, here I am, doing it again. I am, as you like to say, "trying to make art out of everything." But you must know by now that this is how I have survived, that this is how I still survive, this is how I am slowly beginning to believe that perhaps I am not going to die, that perhaps I will grow old. Or at least older.

Readers' Group Guide

1. The introduction states that *"Roar Softly* is a book about how— and what—*women* survive." Yet over the past several decades, sex role distinctions in the Western world have become increasingly blurred. Do you agree that women still face different life challenges than men do? Can you think of any essays in this book that could have been written by a man?

2. What are the drawbacks to pointing out that women and men resolve problems differently? What are the advantages? Is a book (or movie, or magazine) devoted exclusively to women's concerns more likely to help men and women get along better, or to polarize them?

3. Did the content of any of these essays shock or surprise you? If so, which was more startling: the author's experiences, or the fact that she chose to reveal them?

4. Many of the *Roar Softly* writers adopt a lighthearted tone in discussing weighty problems. Why? Does this approach undercut the seriousness of the underlying issues? How does Mary Roach's use of humor in "The Marvels of Middle Age" differ from that of Ms. Gonick in "My Buddies the Oysters"? How, in your experience, does women's use of humor differ from men's?

5. In a sense, each *Roar Softly* essay can be viewed as a mini-memoir—an intimate, first-person narrative about an unusual aspect of the writer's life. What reasons might an author have for writing a memoir? Why, in the alternative, might she choose to transform her experiences into fiction? Can you imagine any

essay in *Roar Softly* recast as a short story or novel? What might the piece gain? What might it lose?

6. Three of the essayists in this book—Cheryl Strayed ("Heroin/e"), Peggy Hong ("Walking the Labyrinth with Mother"), and Edwidge Danticat ("Legends: The Daughter")—write about losing their mothers. How was the loss similar for each author? What factors account for the ways in which it differed?

7. If you had contributed an essay to *Roar Softly*, what challenge in your life would you have chosen to describe? How did you deal with that challenge? Was your approach similar to any of those described in the book?

8. All literary genres require a final resolution—a synthesis, a neat conclusion. To bring about this resolution is part of the writer's art. It's also a feat more easily achieved in fiction: in real life, our problems resist permanent eradication; our experiences are not so easily packaged into tidy little bundles. In which *Roar Softly* essays does the resolution ring true? In which essays do you detect the use of artistic license? Is it possible for a writer to take liberties with the facts of her life, yet still communicate "the truth"? Is it ethical?

9. *Roar Softly* deals, in part, with strategies for resolving personal problems. What would happen if world leaders sought to incorporate the strategies described in this book (Connection, Attitude Adjustment, Mind Over Matter, Problem? What Problem? Perseverance) in resolving social and political problems? Do women leaders use these strategies?

10. What do you think the goal of *Roar Softly* is? Does the book succeed in that goal?

Contributors

Sefi Atta was born in Lagos, Nigeria. She was educated there and in England. A former accountant, she has a master's degree in creative writing from Antioch University, Los Angeles. Her stories have appeared in *In Posse Review*, *Carve*, *Eclectica*, the *Los Angeles Review*, and the *Mississippi Review*. She has won prizes from *Zoetrope* and Red Hen Press and has been short-listed for *Glimmertrain* and Fish Publishing awards. Her radio stories and plays have been broadcast by the BBC and Commonwealth Broadcasting Association. Sefi's first novel, *In the Shadow of Silence* (Interlink Publishing), was a finalist for the Macmillan Writer Prize for Africa.

Gayle Brandeis is the author of *Fruitflesh: Seeds of Inspiration for Women Who Write* and *The Book of Dead Birds: A Novel*, which won Barbara Kingsolver's Bellwether Prize for Fiction in Support of a Literature of Social Change. Her poetry, fiction, and essays have appeared in numerous magazines and anthologies, including Salon.com, *Hip Mama*, and *Nerve*, and have won many awards, including a grant from the Barbara Deming Memorial Fund and the QPB/Story Magazine Short Story Award. She lives in Riverside, California, with her husband and two children.

Anne Burt won Meridian literary magazine's editors' prize in fiction in 2002. She is a commentator for National Public Radio's All Things Considered, and has published essays and fiction in venues including *Working Mother*, Salon.com, *Parenting*, the *Christian Science Monitor*, the *American Book Review*, and elsewhere. She teaches memoir writing at Fordham University and is working on a novel called *The Nightgown Factory*.

Edwidge Danticat is the author of five books including *Breath, Eyes, Memory, Krik? Krak!*, and *The Dew Breaker*. She is also the editor of *The Butterfly's Way: Voices from the Haitian Dyaspora in the United States*.

Jane DeLynn is the author of five novels—*Leash, Don Juan in the Village, Real Estate* (a *New York Times Book Review* Notable Book of the Year), *In Thrall*, and *Some Do*—plus the collection *Bad Sex Is Good*. She was a correspondent in Saudi Arabia for *Mirabella* and *Rolling Stone* during the Gulf War and has published articles, essays, and stories in a number of anthologies and magazines in the United States and abroad, including the *New York Times, Mademoiselle, Glamour, Harper's Bazaar*, the *Paris Review*, the *New York Observer*, and the *Women's Review of Books*. She has written plays and librettos, including the libretto for *The Monkey Opera: The Making of a Soliloquy* (music by Roger Trefousse), which was produced at BAM (the Brooklyn Academy of Music).

Elizabeth Fishel is the author of four nonfiction books: *Sisters, The Men in Our Lives, I Swore I'd Never Do That*, and *Reunion: The Girls We Used To Be, The Women We Became*. She has also written widely for magazines, including *Vogue, Redbook, Family Circle, O, the Oprah Magazine*, and *Ms.*, and has been a contributing editor at *Child*. She has taught writing for many years at the University of California-Berkeley Extension, and privately on Wednesday and Friday mornings. For more information about Wednesday Writers, contact her at erfishel@hotmail.com.

Laura Fraser is a freelance journalist and author, most recently, of *An Italian Affair*, a best-selling travel memoir. She has written for numerous national publications, including *Gourmet, Mother Jones, Health, Vogue, Glamour, Self, Wired*, the *New York Times Magazine, Yoga Journal, Organic Style*, and others. She is also a writing teacher and consultant. A longtime San Franciscan, she operates her own Web site at www.laurafraser.com.

Jane Ganahl has been writing for San Francisco daily newspapers for twenty years. During that time she has covered everything from City Hall to pop music; since 2002, she has been writing the hit column "Single Minded" for the *San Francisco Chronicle*. Her work has also appeared on Salon.com and RollingStone.com and in various magazines, including *Book* and *Parenting*. In her off-hours, she organizes The Last Supper, a monthly dinner salon in San Francisco for creative people, and codirects Litquake, an annual festival of Bay Area literature.

Ms. Gonick writes a weekly column, "Failing at Living," for the *San Francisco Chronicle*. She lives and fails in the Bay Area.

Ariel Gore is Maia's mom and the author of three parenting books— *The Hip Mama Survival Guide*, *The Mother Trip*, and *Whatever, Mom: Hip Mama's Guide to Raising a Teenager*—as well as a novel/memoir, *Atlas of the Human Heart*. When she's not elsewhere, she lives/writes/teaches in Portland, Oregon. You can find her online at www.arielgore.com.

Ayun Halliday is the sole staff member of the quarterly 'zine *The East Village Inky* and the author of *The Big Rumpus: A Mother's Tale from the Trenches* and *No Touch Monkey! And Other Travelers' Lessons Learned Too Late*. She contributes to NPR, *BUST*, *Hip Mama*, and more anthologies than you can shake a stick at without dangling a participle. She lives in Brooklyn, where she's hard at work on her next book, *Job Hopper*. Her website is located at www.ayunhalliday.com.

Cynthia Heimel is the author of *Advanced Sex Tips for Girls: This Time It's Personal*. She has published several volumes of her humorous essays, including *If You Leave Me, Can I Come Too?*; *Get Your Tongue Out of My Mouth, I'm Kissing You Good-bye*; and *If You Can't Live Without Me, Why Aren't You Dead Yet?* She lives in Berkeley with her dogs.

Peggy Hong was born in Seoul, South Korea, and raised in Hawaii and New York. A graduate of Barnard College, she received her MFA in poetry and fiction at Antioch University. She is the author of the poetry chapbooks *The Sister Who Swallows the Ocean* (CrowLadies Press), *Hoofbeats* (Gokiburi Press), and *Lies and Fables* (CrowLadies Press). She is an instructor at Alverno College and lives in Milwaukee, Wisconsin, with her husband and their three teenagers.

Cynthia Kaplan is an actress, comedienne, and author of a collection of essays, *Why I'm Like This: True Stories.* Her work has appeared in the *New York Times*, the *Philadelphia Inquirer*, *New York Magazine*, *Self*, *Health*, *Rosie*, and the journals *Tin House* and *McSweeney's*, among others, and she has contributed essays to the humor collections *More Mirth of a Nation* and *101 Damnations*. She also cowrote and appeared in the film *Pipe Dream*. Kaplan lives in New York City with her husband, son, and daughter, and is working on a second collection of essays to be published by William Morrow whenever she manages to finish it.

Marcelle Karp is proud mama to the tiny wonder, Ruby. Also: a writer, a television producer, a yoga instructor, a knitter, and an insomniac. And, also: the cocreator of the feminist 'zine *Bust*.

Anne Lamott is the author of *Operating Instructions: A Journal of My Son's First Year* and *Bird by Bird: Some Instructions on Writing and Life*, as well as the novels *Hard Laughter*, *Rosie*, *Joe Jones*, *All New People*, and *Crooked Little Heart*. A past recipient of a Guggenheim Fellowship, she lives with her son in northern California.

Meredith Maran is the author of the best-selling books *Dirty: A Search For Answers Inside America's Teenage Drug Epidemic*; *Class Dismissed: A Year in the Life of an American High School, a Glimpse into the Heart of a Nation*; *Ben & Jerry's Double Dip*; and *What It's Like to Live Now*. She also wrote *Notes from An Incomplete Revolution: Real Life Since Feminism* and the children's book *How Would You Feel If Your Dad Was Gay?*, and has published many articles in *Mademoiselle*, *Health*, *Vibe*, the *Utne Reader*, Salon.com, *George*, and *Self*.

Merrill Markoe is a five-time Emmy Award–winning humor writer, columnist, and sometime-performer who has written extensively for many publications, as well as TV and movies. Her sixth and most recent book is *The Psycho Ex Game* (written with Andy Prieboy). She lives in Los Angeles, California, if you can call that living.

Judith Newman is the author of *You Make Me Feel Like an Unnatural Woman: A Diary of a New (Older) Mother*. She writes for *Vanity Fair*, *Discover*, the *New York Times*, and numerous publications here and abroad.

Louise Rafkin lives in Emeryville, California, where she writes and runs Studio Naga, Indonesian Martial Arts and Wellness Center. Her articles and essays have appeared in the *New York Times*, the *Utne Reader*, *Ladies' Home Journal*, the *Los Angeles Times*, and the *Boston Phoenix*. She is the author of *Other People's Dirt: A Housecleaner's Curious Adventures*.

Mary Roach is the author of *Stiff: The Curious Lives of Human Cadavers*, a *New York Times* best-seller and a 2003 pick in the Barnes & Noble Discover Great New Writers Program. Roach's writing has appeared in *Outside*, *Wired*, Salon.com, *GQ*, the *New York Times Magazine*, *The Believer*, and many others. She is a contributing editor at the science magazine *Discover* and was a National Magazine Award Finalist in 1995. She lives in San Francisco with her husband, Ed.

Amy Krouse Rosenthal is the creator/host of the literary and music variety show "Writers' Block Party" on Chicago Public Radio. She is the author of several books, including the forthcoming *Encyclopedia of an Ordinary Life*. She lives in Chicago and in cyberspace at www.mommymommy.com.

Anneli Rufus lives in California and is the author of three books (most recently *Party of One: The Loners' Manifesto*) and the coauthor of five (most recently *California Babylon*).

Autumn Stephens is the author of *Wild Women: Crusaders, Curmudgeons, and Completely Corsetless Ladies in the Otherwise Virtuous Victorian Era,* and six other books in the *Wild Women* series of biography and humor. A former book reviewer for the *San Francisco Chronicle*, she has served as a contributing editor and columnist for *Where* and *SF* magazines. She lives in Berkeley with her husband and two children.

Cheryl Strayed has published fiction and memoirs in *DoubleTake, Nerve,* and *The Sun*, among other magazines, and in several anthologies, including *The Best New American Voices 2003* and twice in *The Best American Essays* (2000 and 2003). The recipient of many awards and residencies, she is a graduate of the MFA program in fiction writing at Syracuse University. Houghton Mifflin will publish her first novel, *Torch*, in 2005.

Joyce Thompson has published ten books with trade and literary presses, nine of them fiction. The tenth, *Sailing My Shoe to Timbuktu* (2003), is a spiritual memoir. She has taught creative writing at every level, from elementary to graduate school. A member of the Writers Guild, West, she has written for screen and stage, and taken part in community theater as both actor and director. Since 1995, she's acted as writer and editorial director for numerous Web sites. She lives in Oakland, where the barrio meets the 'hood, and is inordinately proud of her two children.

Bonnie Wach is the author of *San Francisco As You Like It* and is working on a memoir about her postpartum experience. A former magazine editor, she currently writes columns for the *SF Weekly* newspaper and the *San Francisco Chronicle*. Her work has also appeared in *Health*, the *New York Times Magazine, Travel + Leisure,* and *San Francisco Magazine*. She lives in San Francisco with her husband and son.

Nancy Wartik has written for publications including the *New York Times,* the *Los Angeles Times, Glamour, Self,* and many others. A former staffer at *Ms.* magazine, she has been a contributing editor at *Child*, *Mademoiselle*, and *American Health*. She has taught in the film and media department at Hunter College for the past five years. She lives in New York City with her husband, the writer Dennis Overbye, and her daugher, Mira.

Acknowledgments

Thanks to my friend and publisher, Karen Bouris, who had the vision, and also a damn good title. And to my agent, Amy Rennert, without whom that vision would still be floating in the stratosphere all by its lonesome, sadly unattached to a tangible, you know, book. And to Alma Bune, who, apparently lacking the procrastination gene, always responded to my plaintive e-mails within minutes of the time I sent them.

Thanks to Joyce Thompson and Nancy Wartik, silver and gold, consummate communicators both, for authorial advice, for being my go-to friends. And to Bonnie Wach, a fun date and a fine writer, for hanging in there.

Thanks to Yvonne Mansell and Susan Spiegel for helping me to develop compassion and maintain perspective, for reminding me that I am, in fact, a big brown mountain.

Thanks to Catherine Ference and Marion Reager for countless maternal favors, for camaraderie and *joie de vivre*, for connection.

Thanks to the staff of the afternoon programs at Children's Community Center and Berkwood Hedge School for taking good care of my children while I neglected them to work on this project. And thanks to Jane Friedman, my older son's first grade teacher, for teaching him to write poetry. Here is his Mother's Day poem: *My mommy has a lion in her ear/It's the deadline that made it come/I hope it is over soon/So we can play.*

Thanks to my mother, Yvonne Stephens, for unconditional love, the *sine qua non.*

Thanks to my husband, Keasley Jones, for taking me seriously, and for supporting me in every sense of the phrase.

And thanks, huge heaping quantities of thanks, to the twenty-seven other kindred spirits who contributed to this book. Thanks for your surprising, passionate, humorous, heartbreaking, juicy, witty, sweet, heartfelt prose. Thanks for taking risks, for daring to reveal what is rare and true. Thanks for writing, each of you, according to your own unique style. Thanks for taking (or not) my editorial suggestions with earnestness and grace. The midwife may be useful, but the baby is the miracle. I marvel at you.

Copyright Notices